1

THE SEPARATION OF OWNERSHIP AND CONTROL

THE purpose of this book is to investigate the implications for the theory of the firm of the separation of ownership from control in the large corporation. The theories considered all fall within the general category of managerial theories in that they draw attention to the possibility of the exercise of managerial discretion in the selection of corporate goals. In the static theory the main contributions have been made by W. J. Baumol in *Business Behavior, Value and Growth* and by O. E. Williamson in *The Economics of Discretionary Behavior*. R. M. Cyert and J. G. March in *A Behavioral Theory of the Firm*, with different emphasis, brought some of the concepts of organisation theory into touch with the theory of the firm. In the field of dynamic or growth theory there is predominantly R. L. Marris's *The Economic Theory of 'Managerial' Capitalism*. These works have stimulated much of the development of the theory of the firm in the last few years, and it is one of the purposes of this book to bring together these separate motifs into something resembling a theme.

Part of the justification for this exercise is thus the need to bring recent developments in the theory of the firm into the spectrum of analytical devices available to students of economics: faced with the widely held belief that economists naïvely suppose economic man to be motivated only by monetary or 'material' urges, it is satisfying to be able to point out not only that economists are quite aware of the complexity of human aspirations, but also that they have succeeded in showing that more sophisticated behavioural patterns can be incorporated into the framework of scientific analysis. We can too easily be thrown on to the defensive by practical men.

But the justification for extending the theory of the firm is not in the end that it is intellectually satisfying but that it is necessary for an insight into the nature of contemporary capitalism. An understanding of the relationship between profit, sales, size and growth may enable one to make a more useful contribution to the debate about whether economic and, therefore, political power have passed to a managerial group — distinct from the capitalist or property-owning class — and whether, if they had, this would make any difference to the performance of the firm and therefore of the capitalist system itself. Equally important is the separate but related question of whether the emergence of growth as an objective for the firm and for the economy leads to an increase in well-being. The debate is highly charged with political and policy implications and is far from being a theoretical exercise for its own sake. The purpose here, though, is the limited one of defining more clearly a few of the concepts required by participants.

The pioneer work on the separation of ownership and control is that of Berle and Means.[1] There are four propositions which emerge from their analysis and which may conveniently serve as a point of reference for the present discussion. They suggest first that economic power, in terms of control over physical assets, is tending more and more to concentrate in a few large manufacturing corporations. Second, the assets of large corporations are increasingly under the centralised control of small self-perpetuating groups of professional managers with small personal ownership of the assets they control. Third, the constraints placed upon managerial behaviour by the capital market are increasingly ineffective because of the change in the financial policies of corporations. Fourth, there is a desirable tendency for managers to develop a corporate conscience which leads them to pursue policies quite alien to the raw ethic of entrepreneurial capitalism. This last proposition can clearly be split into three, two of which are in principle empirically verifiable (that managers have consciences which affect their business behaviour) and one (that this is desirable) which is a value judgement with which one might be unable to sympathise.

CONCENTRATION OF WEALTH

Berle's first proposition is the least controversial. His estimate is that whereas in 1929 the one hundred largest American manufacturing corporations controlled 44 per cent of the net capital assets of all manufacturing corporations, in 1962 the figure was 58·4 per cent. The five hundred largest corporations had 70 per cent of the assets. There is some evidence that in the decade up to 1959 the trend was not so clear and that the dominance of large corporations was not increasing, although the dominance itself was evident.[2] However, current work by S. J. Prais at the National Institute of Economic and Social Research confirms that in the United Kingdom there is a strong upward trend in the share in net output of the hundred largest manufacturing enterprises, which has risen from roughly 15 per cent in 1909 to 50 per cent in 1970. On the other hand, if we look at market structure instead of capital assets as an indicator of concentration of wealth, it has been shown by Armstrong and Silberston[3] that concentration increased between 1951 and 1958 in 36 out of 63 trades in British manufacturing. Moreover there is an increasing tendency for the capital outlay of companies to take the form of expenditure on acquisitions: takeovers by non-financial companies in manufacturing, distribution and construction accounted for 4 per cent of capital outlay in 1949–52, for 8 per cent in 1953–8 and for 15 per cent in 1959–66.[4]

OWNERSHIP

Berle draws attention to the changing character of private property and distinguishes individual possessory holdings from 'power systems'. The problems of private property arise where the former gives way to the latter – at the point at which corporate size divorces ownership from control and converts owners into rentiers. He asserts:

'In crude summation, most "owners" own stock, insurance savings and pension claims and the like, and do not manage; most managers (corporate administrators) do not own.'[5]

Florence[6] found evidence of managerial non-ownership in the United Kingdom in the percentage of ordinary shares owned by the board. The median percentage of directors' ordinary holdings in very large companies fell from 2·8 per cent in 1936 to 1·5 per cent in 1951. The results of a study by Villarejo[7] show that the position today in the United States is very similar to that of 1939 when the median holding of officer directors was 1 per cent. It can be seen from Table 1.1 that directors sometimes hold a very small proportion of the ordinary shares of large companies.

Table 1.1[8]

NOMINAL VALUE OF AVERAGE DIRECTOR'S HOLDINGS IN 6 U.K.
COMPANIES WITH ASSETS OF OVER £50 MILLION IN 1951

Company	Assets (£m)	Ordinary share capital (£m)	% of ordinary shares held by board	Nominal value of average director's holding (£)
Lever Bros.	193·7	13·6	23·2	131,466
Imperial Tobacco	123·3	37·6	4·2	46,466
Courtaulds	63·1	24·0	1·2	16,000
British American Tobacco	143·2	23·8	0·2	2,800
Imperial Chemical Industries	236·9	60·6	0·1	3,565
Dunlop Rubber	51·5	12·9	0·03	387

For these six companies the situation in 1971 was as shown in Table 1.2.

Table 1.2

Company	Assets	Ordinary share capital (£m)	% of ordinary shares held by board	Nominal value of average director's holding (£)	Market value of average director's holding (£)
Unilever	825·8	45·8	0·01	216	1,565
Imperial Tobacco	400·2	141·9	0·04	3,400	14,864
Courtaulds	231·4	67·4	0·16	8,508	53,308
British American Tobacco	576·1	59·4	0·01	461	5,996
Imperial Chemical Industries	974·5	468·7	0·02	4,500	11,665
Dunlop Holdings	128·5	48·0	0·04	1,074	5,981

The main difference was that Unilever, Imperial Tobacco and Courtaulds ceased to be dominated by a family interest. The figure for director's holdings includes beneficial interests only; as an example of other interests, 18 per cent of the ordinary shares of Unilever are held by the Leverhulme Trust, operated as a charity.

Evidence of the minute percentage of shares held by the board is unfortunately insufficient to establish the proposition that managers' interests will be different from those of shareholders. More relevant is the proportion of their income which managers derive from their ownership of shares in the companies they run, or, in the absence of information about this, the absolute size of managers' shareholdings. Tables 1.1 and 1.2 give the value of directors' shareholdings for six companies. Recent general evidence is scanty, but Florence's data yield the conclusion that the nominal value of the average director's ordinary share ownership in companies with assets of £3 million or over was some £25,000 in 1936 and £21,000 in 1951. The survey carried out by the Oxford Institute of Statistics[9] found that in 1955 the average value of directors' shareholdings was £28,000. W. G. Lewellen,[10] in a recent study of the rewards of top United States executives based on data from 1940 to 1963, showed that there has been a sharp increase in the value of managerial stockholdings. The market value of average per capita holdings of the executives in the category 'top four after the chief executive' rose from $300,000 in 1953 to $2·3 million in 1963. Such holdings are clearly not insignificant and would certainly not support the contention that managers are a new power group as distinct from shareholders as a whole. Rather does it suggest that the managerial class has either arisen from or joined the capitalist or property-owning class and might be expected to identify with its motives. Marris, in his 1963 analysis of managerial wealth based largely on the Florence data, took the view that

> Managerial stockholding on either the present or even a substantially enhanced scale, while significantly reinforcing the incentive to maintain a reasonable [market valuation], is unlikely to do more than that, is unlikely for example to enforce profit maximisation in the ordinarily understood sense.[11]

Making reasonable assumptions about the relationship between the salaries of corporate officers and the growth of the firm's assets, Marris calculated that the proportion of stock in management's hands would have to rise from 1 per cent to $3\frac{1}{2}$ per cent in order to deter manager-oriented policies on growth. As far as Lewellen's data are concerned, Marris argues[12] that the rise in managerial holdings during 1953–63 was due to special factors such as a change in the United States tax law favouring stock option schemes, and a persistently rising stock market (bull market). The falling market which followed (bear market) caused a resumption of the net selling which had been taking place, on Lewellen's evidence, from 1940 to 1953. Furthermore, the United Kingdom trends may be different from those in the United States: evidence covering the last ten years is lacking. Still, the

Lewellen results are, on any interpretation, a compelling reason for refusing to accept any simple hypothesis about managerial independence of the stock market.

CONTROL

Whatever the degree of correspondence of interest between managers and shareholders, as long as the correspondence is less than complete it will be necessary to investigate the extent to which shareholders can ensure that corporate assets are managed in their interest. Attention therefore shifts to a consideration of the conditions existing in the capital market to which management will have to go for funds for expansion. Even if conditions in output markets are monopolistic and therefore productive of rent elements in the earnings of corporations, imperfections in the capital market will be a necessary condition for the exercise of managerial discretion. Competitive capital markets would guarantee the management of resources in such a way that the rents accrued to the owners of those resources rather than to the managers of them. According to E. V. Rostow:

> The current prototype increasingly is that of a corporation with stock widely scattered amongst individuals, investment trusts or institutional investors who faithfully vote for the incumbent management and resolutely refuse to participate in its concerns.[13]

The non-participation of British institutions in the affairs of companies in which they hold significant interests is well known. It is interesting that the Bank of England has recently increased its efforts to persuade them to play a more active role in the hope that the efficiency of British industry will be improved if the capital market is less complacent.[14]

Berle's criterion for management control was that no individual or small group should possess more than 20 per cent of the voting stock, otherwise it could be classified as minority control. However, in none of the firms classed as management-controlled was the dominant group in fact in possession of more than 5 per cent of the voting stock. In other words the proposition is that a firm may be assumed to be controlled by its managers if no identifiable group of shareholders can exert concerted pressure on them. By this criterion, between 1929 and

1963, among the two hundred largest non-financial American corporations the number classed as management-controlled had risen from 88 to 169, representing respectively 58 per cent and 85 per cent of their combined wealth.

The suitability of Berle's criterion is clearly open to challenge. For example, Beed[15] argues that only an examination of the actual behaviour of firms could reveal whether in practice management was free from outside influence or not and that no significance should be attached to arbitrary percentages of voting stock. He makes the point that widely dispersed ownership could just as well deliver control into the hands of anyone acquiring only a small percentage of votes as make it difficult, as Berle suggests, for any small group to get sufficient votes for control.

There are two related questions here. First, what evidence is there of passive acquiescence by owners? Second, to what extent do the financial policies (i.e. their choice of methods of raising funds) reflect such passivity? This second question will be considered in the next section (p. 12 below).

Concerning the first question, shareholder oversight will tend to be incomplete because imperfect information will reinforce natural inertia. Knauth[16] claims that in order to be safe from shareholders' vigilance the degree of success required from managements is small: 'Management must fail obviously and even ignominiously before the dispersed forces of criticism become mobilised for action.'

The directors are elected at the annual shareholders' meeting which it is in practice impossible for most of them to attend. The right to vote has in reality become the right to choose whom to nominate as one's proxy. Shareholder apathy normally ensures that proxy votes will be returned to the offices of the corporation and used by the management. If dissatisfaction with the management is felt by a minority group of shareholders, whether this group was formerly in control of the management or is attempting to gain control, it will have to set in motion the expensive process of circulating shareholders and bidding for their support by returning alternative proxies. The proxy machinery, which in principle ensures the absent shareholder some control, is in practice one of the chief means of depriving him of such control.

A test used by O. E. Williamson[17] to support Knauth's claim considers the performance of companies for which intention to wage a proxy contest was filed with the United States Securities and

Exchange Commission from 1956 to 1964. 32 per cent of these companies showed negative profits in two of the last three years and 53 per cent were paying zero cash dividends. In a random sample of comparable firms the proportions were 13 per cent and 20 per cent. The implication is that the performance of firms whose managements are threatened is very much worse than that of the average firm – not perhaps a very surprising result. Perhaps equally interesting is the fact that so many managements are allowed to do so badly without being challenged. The analysis assumes that filing a statement can be taken as an indicator that the capital market has become an active rather than a passive constraint. Beed's view, based on Australian data, is that the insulation of directors from owners is by no means complete. Since 15 per cent of votes is typically sufficient to secure re-election, the outcome could well be determined by a small number of large owners who do not necessarily automatically approve of the board's policies. Normally, in the absence of dispute, the existing directors will obtain the proxy votes of large owners, the effect being 'a disfranchisement of the vast majority of minute owners in the individual company rather than a total separation of ownership from control.'[18] But at the same time it is doubtful if management could withstand the disapproval of the large owners if its policies were either unsuccessful or insufficiently owner-oriented.

Given that it is difficult in practice for existing shareholders to unseat directors at the annual meeting, the question arises whether the possibility of their taking legal action represents a potential threat to the board. In the United States the stockholder suit is intended to protect the corporation (i.e. the shareholders?) against fraud and other breaches of duty on the part of officers and directors. Rostow considers this course of action to be costly and ineffective. Even more significantly, even in the United States both statute and case law treat as dubious practice the stockholder suit against managers who misuse the funds entrusted to them. In Britain dissident shareholders would not go to the courts at all but would (if they did not sell their shares) either form a shareholders' committee, the very existence of which would put pressure on the board, or request the Department of Trade and Industry to appoint inspectors to investigate the company's affairs. This rarely happens.

Apart from the control exercised by existing shareholders, there is the potential danger of a take-over bid – an attempted acquisition of sufficient voting stock for control by an individual or group with a wide variety of motives. The effect on existing management is likely to be at best that they are forced to change their policies and at worst that they will be replaced. This threat from raiders plays an important part in *Managerial Capitalism,* but the emphasis there is upon the scarcity of raiders in contrast with the traditional assumption that challenges to existing managements will occur with terrible swiftness whenever the rate of return they are producing is less than the market rate of discount, which is the opportunity cost to investors of leaving their funds where they are. No assessment of the likely relevance of raiders is made in *Managerial Capitalism,* except for the implication that the threat will form a prominent feature of the landscape in which decisions are made.

O. E. Williamson[19] argues that the raider threat is small on the grounds that:

(*a*) the proxy machinery favours existing management;
(*b*) the performance of raider managements often fails to meet expectations; and
(*c*) raiders' motives are regarded with suspicion by the market.

The last suggestion is borne out by Rostow, who claims that the raider is increasingly unacceptable in spite of the fact that he is exercising historic legal rights and is encouraging the proper allocation of scarce resources. Raiding is thought to be a particularly reprehensible breach of business propriety if the challenge comes from those who wish to acquire voting stock, i.e. control, rather than being solely interested in an increased rate of dividend: in many cases, he claims, acquisition for voting purposes is illegal in the United States. However, since Rostow wrote (1959) there has been an increase in take-overs in the United States. Raiders may be active in spite of the suspicion with which they are regarded. British practice does not reflect the same kind of management-inspired sense of decorum. The acquisition of stock for the purpose of voting is normal. Some restraint upon the behaviour of raiders is to be found in the City Take-over Code, where the emphasis is upon protecting the rights of shareholders: for example, if an offer is made all existing shareholders must be offered exactly the same terms. In these circumstances the distinction between acquiring shares for voting purposes and acquiring them for income or capital gain becomes difficult to justify.

The importance of take-over and the fear of take-over in encouraging boards to maximise profits has been investigated by Singh[20] in an analysis of companies quoted on the London stock exchange from 1955 to 1960. Several conclusions may be drawn from the study:

1. Take-over occurs on a large enough scale for it to be a significant element in any explanation of business behaviour. Of the 2,126 firms engaged in manufacturing industry (excluding steel) which were quoted on the United Kingdom exchanges in 1954, more than 400 had been acquired by 1960. This does not take account of the smaller unquoted companies among whom the incidence of take-over may well be higher.

2. When taken-over companies are compared with those not taken over, it is found that, of the variables which might have been expected to reveal interesting divergences (profitability, size, market valuation, liquidity, gearing, retention ratio and growth), only the first two in fact did so. In the case of size there was no simple tendency for the probability of take-over to decrease as size increased. Instead there were erratic changes from one size category to the next. However, for firms in the largest size category (assets over £4 million) there was a much smaller likelihood of being taken over and a clearer tendency for the probability of take-over to fall with increasing size (see Table 1.3). As for profitability, the overall probability of being taken

Table 1.3[21]

Size (£m)	Number of companies	% taken over
4 to 8	59	13·5
8 to 16	30	6·6
Over 16	15	0

over within a year was 3·8 per cent: for the most profitable firms the profitability was 1·7 per cent and for the least profitable 7·4 per cent. In a sense, therefore, one could say that a very profitable firm is decidedly less likely to be taken over than an unprofitable one, although some highly profitable firms are in fact taken over. On the other hand, in absolute terms there is a very small probability of being taken over within a year in any case and it is arguable that the difference is unimportant. If one set out to spot the firms which would be taken over in the coming year, random selection of 100 companies would yield about 4 victims whereas 100 selected from the least profitable companies would yield about 7. In both cases one would be wrong nearly all the time!

3. Justifying Williamson's second point, there is no evidence that new managements increase the profitability of assets after take-over. In each of the five industries selected (food, drink, clothing and footwear, electrical engineering and non-electrical engineering) over half the acquiring companies fared worse than the rest of the industry, at least in the first two years after take-over.

The profitability point is reinforced by Rose and Newbould:

> The evidence provided by our 1967 sample does not support the thesis that it is a distinct characteristic of the majority of companies being acquired to have a rate of return that is relatively low for the industry concerned.[22]

In general one might therefore question whether mergers contribute to efficiency by replacing less able managements with more able ones. While the take-over threat may put pressure on management to improve performance, take-over itself may merely be a wasteful reshuffling of the managerial pack, which reduces efficiency instead of increasing it.

Two further points from Singh's study are worth mentioning in any assessment of the extent of managerial insulation from capital-market influence. First, the wide variation in profitability between industries and between firms in the same industry indicates that market forces, of which take-over is a part, are a long way from ensuring the complete erosion of managerial discretion. Second, although one may assume the fear of take-over is a real constraint upon management, the actual event is not necessarily a disaster in the sense that managers of taken-over firms are not necessarily fired. On the other hand the uncertainty is a considerable fear. Whatever the size or profitability of the acquired firm, half of the directors will be fired within two years and it will not be certain which they will be. Furthermore, the future of the other half is also uncertain in the long run. The question is whether fear of take-over is based on a realistic assessment of the consequences of inefficiency or is a widespread fear little related to performance. The relationship between take-over and market valuation is discussed again in Chapter 7.

FINANCIAL POLICY

It remains to consider the financial policies of managers with respect to (a) the necessity to have recourse to the market for funds and (b) their willingness to take account of shareholders' relative preferences for dividends and retentions.

(a) According to Berle the origin of finance capital has changed. A mature corporation typically does not rely on investor-supplied capital, in the sense of new issues of stock. More than 60 per cent of capital is internally generated, that is, 'price-generated'; 20 per cent is borrowed from banks; rather less than 20 per cent is individual savings – mainly through issuing bonds to intermediaries such as life insurance companies and pension funds. This would imply a virtual nullifying of the mechanism by which savings are allocated to their most efficient uses through changes in the cost of capital to the corporation. However, Lintner claims that the expected greater reliance on internally generated funds has not occurred and that the ratio of internal to external funds is stable. Furthermore, whatever the growth in their discretionary power has been, corporations are arriving at decisions in financing which pay due regard to the relative cost of the various sources of funds:

> Profitability and the pressure of increasing sales are still the dominant determinants of investment outlays – as they should be in a free enterprise economy – and the relative rates of expansion of assets and physical investments among industries as well as among firms is markedly associated with relative rates of profitability in accordance with standard market criteria.[23]

(b) Lintner has found elsewhere[24] that dividends (rather than retained earnings) were the primary and active decision variable in most situations. Savings by firms in a given period were largely a by-product of dividend action taken in terms of pretty well established practices and policies; dividends were rather seldom a by-product of current decisions regarding the desired magnitudes of savings as such.[25] However, fixed percentage payout was not common: in most firms consideration of what dividend should be paid at any given time turned on the question of whether the existing rate of payment should be changed. There would be serious consideration of just how large the change in individual payments should be only after management had satisfied itself that a change in the existing rate would be positively desirable. Even then the existing dividend rate continued to be the central point of reference for the problem.

By far the most important factor influencing the desirability and the amount of any change in the dividend was the level of current net earnings. Their suitability as a criterion arises from the fact that they are widely reported in the financial press and that management would expect shareholders and the financial community generally to be aware of them and to find them significant. Most officers and directors regarded their stockholders as having a proprietary interest in earnings and believed that, unless there were other compelling reasons to the contrary, their fiduciary responsibilities and standards of fairness required them to distribute part of any substantial increase in earnings to the stockholders in dividends. Even executives who were most inclined to view the interests of the company as distinct from those of the shareholders and who seemed least concerned to frame dividend policy in the best interests of the shareholders as such, were generally concerned with the decline in favourable proxies and with the weakening of their personal positions which they believed would follow if dividends failed to reflect a fair share of increased earnings.

The relationship between current earnings and the existing dividend rate therefore determined the amount of any change decided upon. Most firms had an ideal or *target ratio* of dividends to current earnings towards which they would move. Their formal policy was that dividends should be adjusted by some fraction of the difference between last period's payment and the rate which would be indicated by applying the target payout ratio to current earnings. The target ratios varied from 20 per cent to 80 per cent with 50 per cent the most common figure and most of the rest aiming at 40 per cent or 60 per cent. With respect to speed of adjustment, most firms sought to move some part of the way within each year, with the fraction made up in each year varying from one-half to as little as one-sixth. Thus some further increases in current dividends are to be expected, even in years when profits suffer some decline, whenever substantial earlier increases in earnings have not yet been fully reflected in dividends and the existing rates are still below target payout ratios applied to the new (lower) rate of earnings. The partial adaptation mechanism means that dividends act as a buffer to the shocks of cyclical movements in the environment.

The target ratios observed by Lintner agree with Berle's 1967 estimate of 60 per cent as the typical payout ratio. However, Baumol's[26] observations are somewhat at variance with Lintner's. Baumol agrees that profits should be divided between dividends and reinvestment in a manner which takes shareholders' preferences and interests into account; in fact he goes further and judges that in principle the division should be that which most closely accords with stockholder preferences. He agrees that dividends are the decision variable for managers because they are accepted as an index of success by the market. He suggests that the value of shares is more closely correlated with dividends than with retained earnings. But he believes that firms retain more than shareholders wish, a practice not in accord with the attitudes of Lintner's most well-behaved managers. On the other hand, even they do not pay exclusive attention to shareholders' preference for current dividend income as compared with longer-term capital gains: to judge by market-price fluctuation, it seems that most large companies at most times have indeed paid smaller dividends than stockholders would have preferred.[27] Management's assessment of this preference is only one of a long list of factors determining the target payout ratio. In other words, although the dividend is undoubtedly the focal point of the decision-making, there is no suggestion that shareholders' own criterion for determining their own welfare is the only basis for policy. Among the more important other factors mentioned by Lintner were: the growth prospects of the company and the industry; the average cyclical movement of investment opportunities, working capital requirements and internal cash flows; management's views of shareholder preference between reasonably stable or fluctuating dividend rates, and its judgement of the size of any premium the market might put on stability or stable growth in the dividend rate; the normal payouts of competitive companies; the financial strength of the company and its policy on the use of debt and new equity issues; and its confidence in the soundness of earnings figures as reported by its accounting department.

In Chapters 6 and 7 we consider the choice of payout ratio or retention ratio in theoretical situations where many of the practical considerations mentioned by Lintner are 'smoothed' away. On the assumptions made there, shareholder welfare should not be affected by the choice between retentions and new issues of shares as the method of financing a given rate of growth. Baumol is of course not alone in observing that shareholders seem in practice to prefer dividends to retained earnings, probably because in an uncertain world a dividend now is the most reliable form of reward.

The tentative conclusion is that Berle was probably wrong in asserting that capital-market constraints are becoming increasingly ineffective. Although managers have considerable latitude, the capital market cannot be ignored: indeed there is a strong suggestion that managers' attitude to shareholders is much more positive than the term 'constraint' would imply.

MANAGERIAL REVOLUTION, TECHNOSTRUCTURE AND CORPORATE CONSCIENCE

Galbraith[28] has put the predominance of managers and managerial goals into historical perspective. He points out that until the nineteenth century power rested with the owners of land, but that during that century it passed to capital because this emerged as the factor of production which was hardest to obtain and to replace. Just as it had been impossible for Ricardo and Malthus to conceive of a system in which land had lost its strategic position, so in the last fifty years has the body of economic theory been reluctant to accept the dethronement of capital. This reluctance may be attributed to a belief that traditional forces are both more natural and more beneficial:

> We may lay it down as a rule that the older the exercise of any power the more benign it will appear and the more recent its assumption the more unnatural and even dangerous it will seem.[29]

The shift of power from capital to what Galbraith calls the technostructure has been disguised because the pre-eminence of capital is believed to be immutable and because power has not passed to another established factor of production. In fact, given a competent business organisation, capital is now ordinarily available, whereas technical expertise is more scarce. It is questionable whether Galbraith has in fact demonstrated that, in his own terminology, the supply of organised intelligence is more inelastic at the margin than the supply of capital. However, one would not deny the shift of power itself; the argument is about the extent of the shift.

Power, then, has not passed to labour, the next candidate among traditional factor classifications, which has some limited authority over pay and working conditions but none over the enterprise, and which is in any case relatively abundant. It has not passed to the classical entrepreneur, who is a diminishing figure in the industrial system. It has passed to:

> the association of men of diverse technical knowledge, experience or other talent which modern industrial technology and planning require. It extends from the leadership of the modern industrial enterprise down to just short of the labour force and embraces a large number of people and a large variety of talent.[30]

The technological and managerial revolutions have produced, according to Galbraith, a technostructure whose aim is to make sufficient profit to secure the independent life of the organisation, to achieve maximum rate of growth of the organisation and to produce things which are challenging to technological ingenuity. Whereas in the orthodox market economy consumers' preferences indicate what producers should produce, in the revised Galbraith sequence producers design future products, plan ahead their quantities and prices, and then mould consumer taste to take up these products. The objectives of the technostructure have damaging effects upon the well-being of the community because the growth of output of physical products is pursued regardless of the social costs of pollution and congestion. Higher levels of material consumption are preferred to more leisure.

The relationship between growth and welfare is an extremely complex one involving basic value judgements and is too important to be summarised in a few words. One would only point out that it is not necessarily the case that damage done to the environment (and therefore to one section of the population) by the production and consumption of certain goods causes an amount of unhappiness which outweighs the benefits conferred upon other sections. While there is probably in the long run a point where the increasing costs and the diminishing benefits of greater growth would indicate some kind of optimum level of 'material' production, the unanswered question is whether we are at such a point already. As Crosland says: 'Generally, those enjoying an above-average standard of living should be rather chary of admonishing those less fortunate on the perils of material riches.'[31]

Meade[32] has challenged much of Galbraith's thesis and in particular what he calls the latter's economic determinism. Galbraith says:

> The imperatives of organisation, technology and planning operate similarly on all societies. Given the decision to have modern industry, much of what happens is inevitable and the same.[33]

Meade agrees with Galbraith that some counterweight to the influence of the technostructure is desirable, but argues that the trends observed in 'The New Industrial State' are not inevitable and that in any case it is possible, through a combination of public ownership, government intervention, national indicative planning and free enterprise, to control the technostructure and maintain the ultimate sovereignty of the individual citizen. For one thing, the technostructure, though responsible for a great deal of economic activity, has left unscathed large parts of the modern economic system.[34] For another, it is possible that, in future, consumption expenditures will be switched to the products of the tertiary sector — hotels, travel, entertainments, etc. — and to specialised luxury products, rather than to industrial products. It would thus be wrong to assume that what Meade calls 'the liberal forces of profit-maximising competition' did not still have an important part to play.

When it comes to positive action for the reinforcement of the constraints of the market mechanism, Meade has five suggestions:

1. A substantial tax on advertising, which would increase the incentive to seek markets by cutting prices and costs, discourage wasteful competitive advertising and ease conditions of entry.
2. State promotion of consumers' research and education.
3. A free trade area in all industrial products of all highly industrialised countries, so as to stimulate competitive forces.
4. Company taxation which discriminates against retentions and in favour of dividends.
5. The creation of a free market in new methods through government promotion of research and development, the results to be freely available to all producers.

Finally, Meade challenges Galbraith's belief that one can have either planning or a market-price mechanism but not both. The admitted in-

creased need for careful forward planning in a system which involves
the commitment of large resources to inflexible uses over long periods
of time is accompanied by an increased need for a price mechanism,

> that is to say, for reliance on a system of prices as a signalling
> device to indicate to producers and consumers what is and what is
> not scarce. This arises because input–output relationships have
> become so complex and the differentiation between products so
> manifold that simple quantitative planning without a price or
> market mechanism becomes increasingly clumsy and inefficient.[35]

Berle's vision of the future is entirely different. He sees the corporation as a socially unifying force comparable to the church in the Mid-
dle Ages and predicts that it may supersede the state as the dominant
form of social organisation. The managers having broken the tradition
that the corporation be operated solely for the benefit of the passive
owners, Berle agrees with everyone else that society's interest must be
taken into account. But his solution is almost unbelievably naïve and,
it seems to me, horrifying:

> It is conceivable – indeed it seems almost essential if the corporate
> system is to survive – that the 'control' of the great corporations
> should develop into a purely neutral technocracy, balancing a
> variety of claims by various groups in the community and assigning
> to each a portion of the income stream on the basis of public policy
> rather than private cupidity.[36]

Even worse,

> Management thus becomes, in an odd sort of way, the uncontrolled
> administrator of a kind of trust having the privilege of perpetual ac-
> cumulation. The stockholder is the passive beneficiary.[37]

The chairman of Standard Oil can claim that the managers of his
company conduct its affairs

> in such a way as to maintain an equitable and working balance
> among the claims of the various directly interested groups –
> stockholders, employees, customers and the public at large.[38]

In the view of Kaysen:

> No longer the agent of proprietorship seeking to maximise return on
> investment, management sees itself as responsible to stockholders,

employees, customers, the general public, and, perhaps most important, the firm itself as an institution. . . . Its responsibilities to the general public are widespread: leadership in local charitable enterprise, concern with factory architecture and landscaping, provision of support for higher education, and even research in pure science, to name a few.[39]

Galbraith has an even more formidable assortment of secondary goals:

> Building a better community; improved education; better understanding of the free enterprise system; an effective attack on heart ailments, emphysema, alcoholism, hard chancre or other crippling disease; participation in the political party of choice; and renewed emphasis on regular religious observances.[40]

Even Crosland, from a position slightly left of centre in the British political spectrum, welcomes the change in the rules of business behaviour and the absence of traditional capitalist ruthlessness. He does, however, reject the concept of joint responsibility to workers, shareholders, customers and the public as 'ambivalent and potentially contradictory': 'The objective remains high profits and rapid growth. It is pursued, it is true, in a more civilised and less aggressive manner.'[41]

The view taken by Berle and Galbraith of managerial objectives is one which will not, on the whole, be pursued here. There is, in the nature of things, little evidence that managers have consciences except from their own pronouncements. In any case, if the instruments of production are to be operated for the general rather than the particular benefit, it is arguable that the proper agents of the general will should be in some sense generally accountable: certainly the proposition that managers are free from the pressing constraints of market forces does not imply that they will or should develop consciences along with their freedom. While one might be prepared to agree that subordinate goals of the kind mentioned are present, one would regard them as an intolerable encroachment of the sectional ethic of businessmen into economic and social areas which should concern them only as individual citizens; and they lead to a misallocation of resources because neither the corrective of market forces nor that of collective choice is at work.

Therefore, of the above-mentioned responsibilities of managers, only two will be assumed relevant for the present analysis: shareholders and 'the firm itself'. The rest are either very subordinate goals or they are the proper concern of other bodies, chiefly government. The assumption of a 'stockholder-oriented conscience', in Marris's phrase, is in general justified on the ground that, even in terms of the nominal value of their shareholding in their own companies, large corporation directors are men of property. This does not imply that managers consciously identify with shareholders on the basis of social class in a way which might conflict with their interest as managers. But it does suggest a basis for a reasonable guess at the kind of elements which might form the constituents of a managerial utility function.

The Berlian propositions with which this chapter began have been neither established nor refuted. There is no consensus on the extent of managerial independence. The evidence is inconclusive or contradictory, and one's interpretation of it therefore relies heavily on the technique of selecting those portions which fit preconceptions formed because they are either analytically or politically convenient. Some of the more relevant issues having been given an airing, what can be said? Managers identify to an unagreed extent with shareholders. In a situation where conflict arises, managers are constrained to a disputed degree by the capital market. Capital-market control works through the vote at the general meeting, through the freedom to sell shares and depress the market price, and through managerial fear of take-over. The relative importance of these varies.

NOTES AND REFERENCES

1. A. A. Berle and G. C. Means, *The Modern Corporation and Private Property,* rev. ed. (New York: Harcourt, Brace & World, 1967).

2. J. Lintner, 'The Financing of Corporations', in E. S. Mason (ed.), *The Corporation in Modern Society* (Cambridge, Mass.: Harvard Univ. Press, 1959) p. 170.

3. A. G. Armstrong and A. Silberston, 'Size of Plant, Size of Enterprise and Concentration in British Manufacturing Industry 1935–58', *Journal of the Royal Statistical Society,* vol. cxxviii, 3 (1965) p. 404.

4. H. B. Rose and G. D. Newbould, 'The 1967 Take-over Boom', *Moorgate and Wall Street* (autumn 1967). Both this and the previous reference are cited in R. M. Cyert and K. D. George, 'Competition, Growth and Efficiency', *Economic Journal* (Mar. 1969) p. 25. See also note 34 below.

5. Berle and Means, *The Modern Corporation*, p. x (Preface).

6. P. Sargant Florence, *Ownership, Control and Success of Large Companies* (London: Sweet & Maxwell, 1961).

7. D. Villarejo, 'Stock Ownership and the Control of Corporations', *New University Thought* (Chicago, 1961, 1962).

8. T. Nichols, *Ownership, Control and Ideology* (London: Allen & Unwin, 1969) p. 76.

9. L. R. Klein *et al.*, 'Savings and Finances of the Upper Income Classes', *Bulletin of the Oxford Institute of Statistics* (Nov. 1956) p. 308.

10. W. G. Lewellen, *The Ownership Income of Management* (New York: Columbia Univ. Press, 1971).

11. R. L. Marris, *The Economic Theory of 'Managerial' Capitalism* (London: Macmillan, 1964) p. 77.

12. Review of Lewellen, *The Ownership Income of Management*, in *Journal of Economic Literature* (June 1972).

13. E. V. Rostow, 'To Whom is Corporate Management Responsible?', in Mason (ed.), *The Corporation in Modern Society*, p. 53.

14. An interesting contemporary case study in the involvement of the institutions is provided by the pressure brought by them upon the Distillers Company in the United Kingdom to raise their compensation offer to children suffering from the effects of the drug thalidomide. The case also, of course, raises wider issues of managerial and shareholder motivation, and is not so much about efficiency as about the extent of a corporation's responsibility for 'externalities'.

15. C. S. Beed, 'The Separation of Ownership from Control', *Journal of Economic Studies*, vol. I, no. 2 (1966). Reprinted in M. Gilbert (ed.) *The Modern Business Enterprise* (Harmondsworth: Penguin Books 1972).

16. O. Knauth, *Managerial Enterprise: Its Growth and Methods of Operations* (New York: W. W. Norton, 1948) p. 45.

17. A. Phillips and O. E. Williamson (eds.), *Prices: Issues in Theory, Practice and Public Policy* (Oxford Univ. Press, 1969) p. 13.

18. Beed, op. cit., p. 31.

19. O. E. Williamson, *The Economics of Discretionary Behavior* (Chicago: Markham, 1967) p. 23.

20. A. Singh, *Take-overs* (Cambridge Univ. Press, 1971); summarised in W. B. Reddaway, 'An Analysis of Take-overs', *Lloyds Bank Review* (Apr. 1972).

21. Reddaway, op. cit., p. 14.

22. Rose and Newbould, op. cit.

23. Lintner, op. cit., p. 190.

24. J. Lintner, 'Distribution of Incomes of Corporations among Dividends, Retained Earnings and Taxes', *American Economic Association, Papers and Proceedings* (May 1956).

25. This suggestion, together with its implication that the 'target' retention ratio (see below, p. 13) is unrelated to the desired growth rate (see Chapter 6), does not accord with impressionistic evidence that dividend policies are closely related to the needs of finance for growth. In Lintner's contribution to *The Corporate Economy* (ed. R. L. Marris and A. J. B. Wood (London: Macmillan, 1971)), 'Optimum or Maximum Corporate Growth under Uncertainty', the target retention ratio is specifically related to the growth rate.

26. W. J. Baumol, *Business Behavior, Value and Growth* (New York: Macmillan, 1959) p. 52.

27. Lintner, 'The Financing of Corporations', p. 172.

28. J. K. Galbraith, *The New Industrial State* (London: Hamish Hamilton, 1967).

29. Ibid., p. 56. It is entirely arguable, of course, that capital has not in fact been

dethroned. But Galbraith dismisses with a wave of the pen the Marxist argument that, in spite of superficial evidence of change, capital remains a controlling force. As far as economic theory is concerned, R. Dorfman, for example, points out ('An Economic Interpretation of Optimal Control Theory', *American Economic Review,* Dec. 1969) that in the last decade capital theory has received a new lease of life through the application to it of the modern version of the calculus of variations, referred to currently as 'optimal control theory' (Pontryagin and all that). Dorfman says: 'As a result, capital theory has become so profoundly transformed that it has been rechristened growth theory.' If capital theory may be equated with growth theory it is difficult to argue, as Galbraith does, that the abundance of capital deprives it of any decisive role.

30. Galbraith, *The New Industrial State,* p. 59.

31. C. A. R. Crosland, *The Future of Socialism,* rev. ed. (London: Cape, 1964) p. 222.

32. J. E. Meade, 'Is "The New Industrial State" Inevitable?', *Economic Journal* (June 1968).

33. Galbraith, *The New Industrial State,* p. 396.

34. Meade is not of course alone in pointing out the importance of the 'other' sectors of the economy. (See G. C. Allen, 'Economic Fact and Fantasy' *Occasional Paper No. 14* (London: Institute of Economic Affairs, 1969)). Support can be found in O. E. Williamson's *Corporate Control and Business Behavior* (Englewood Cliffs, N.J.: Prentice-Hall, 1970), in which he defines 'giant' firms as the 25 largest industrials, the 10 largest utilities and the 10 largest transport undertakings – firms with assets in 1967 of more than $2 billion. These giants account for 40 per cent of the receipts of the industrial sector, 60 per cent of receipts in utilities and 50 per cent in transport. Of the 40 per cent of national income and employment attributable to these sectors, large firms accounted for half, giants for almost a quarter. Williamson concludes:

'Although these are not trivial proportions, they do not clearly constitute dominance. Even allowing for significant 'leadership' by the large-firm core, . . . it is presumptuous to suggest that an analysis which focuses on these large firms is addressed to *most* of what is relevant in the American economy. To claim that it is concerned with *much* of what is relevant is, however, sufficient for our purpose.' (Ibid., p. 8.)

35. Meade, op. cit., p. 391.

36. Berle and Means, *The Modern Corporation,* p. 313.

37. Ibid., p. xv (Preface).

38. E. S. Mason, 'The Apologetics of Managerialism', *Journal of Business* (Jan. 1958).

39. C. Kaysen, 'The Social Significance of the Modern Corporation', *American Economic Association, Papers and proceedings* (May 1957).

40. Galbraith, *The New Industrial State,* p. 176. But for the opposite face of the corporation, see note 14 above.

41. C. A. R. Crosland, 'The Private and Public Corporation in Great Britain', in Mason Ed.), *The Corporation in Modern Society,* p. 267.

2

THE CONTRIBUTION OF ORGANISATION THEORY

THE firm viewed as an organisation rather than as an abstraction is a coalition of sub-groups whose individual goals are inherently contradictory. The classical theory of the firm assumes that the ownership group determines the behaviour of the firm: persons in other groups are provided with opportunity-cost returns – what Cyert and March[1] term 'side-payments'. After the side-payments are made all conflict is settled. The entrepreneur has an objective; he purchases whatever services he needs to achieve the objective. In return for such payments employees contract to perform whatever is required of them. For a price the employee adopts the organisation goal.

But to the organisation theorist the foregoing is an asymmetrical description of the coalition because it categorises wages as a cost or side-payment whereas dividends are profit which is considered a policy commitment. This emphasis on the asymmetry has seriously confused the understanding of organisational goals:

> Ultimately it makes only slightly more sense to say that the goal of a business organisation is to maximise profit than to say that its goal is to maximise the salary of the caretaker's assistant.[2]

There are, in fact, good reasons for regarding some coalition members as different from others: for instance, many shareholders are passive most of the time, so that the payment demands they make may be rather easily met. The Cyert and March point is that the old distinction between policy commitments on the one hand and monetary side-payments on the other is becoming blurred by the trend towards policy side-payments – for example, trade unions entering what has been viewed traditionally as the management prerogative of policy-making and demanding payments in that area. As they put it:

Side-payments, far from being the incidental distribution of a fixed, transferable booty, represent the central process of goal specification. That is, a significant number of these payments are in the form of policy commitments.

Policy commitments are thus an important part of the method by which coalitions are formed. In the process of bargaining over side-payments many of the organisational goals are defined or clarified. It is however arguable that the concepts of side-payment and policy commitment serve only to confuse the issue and that blurring the distinction between them makes matters worse.

The five goals selected as sufficient out of the large number which could conceivably be relevant to price, output and sales strategy decisions are:

1. Production goal with two major components: a smoothing goal and a level of production goal.
2. Inventory goal either in terms of an absolute level or a range.
3. Sales goal in terms either of value or of physical volume or both.
4. Market shares goal as an alternative to (3) as a measure of sales effectiveness.
5. Profit goal, which summarises the demand for accumulating resources in order to distribute them in the form of capital investments, dividends, payments to creditors or increased budgets to sub-units; or, alternatively, as a measure of performance for top management.

These objectives are in some cases conflicting and inconsistent, and the eradication of inconsistencies would be a necessary prerequisite for rational decision-making, that is, decision-making designed to achieve some clearly formulated goal. This is the sense in which rationality has normally been defined in economic theory, and there would seem to be no good reason for abandoning this meaning. Economic Man was never thought of as an individual who could obtain satisfaction only from marketable commodities but rather as an individual who, having specified his objectives, only took actions consistent with their achievement.

It is not so in the case of Organisation Man. The goals enumerated by Cyert and March have the following characteristics:

(a) They are imperfectly rationalised. New demands are not necessarily consistent with existing policies but this inconsistency may fail to be discovered.

(*b*) Some objectives are stated in the form of aspiration-level constraints rather than maximising constraints. In a steady state,
aspiration levels tend to exceed achievement by a small amount:
where achievement increases at an increasing rate, aspiration
level will exhibit short-run lags behind achievement; where
achievement decreases, aspiration level would be above achievement.

Thus the theory of organisational behaviour must allow not only for
conflicting objectives but also for the possibilities that objectives will
change with experience and that not all objectives or all demands will
receive attention at the same time – a phenomenon referred to as shifts
in attention focus. In other words, the organisation can remain viable
by attending to demands in sequence. At the same time the organisation will try to solve problems of unsatisfactory performance and the
consequent increase in inter-group conflict by:

(*a*) uncertainty avoidance;
(*b*) problemistic search – that is, search which is motivated by a
problem and which proceeds to more complex possibilities for
solution only as simple ones fail; and
(*c*) organisational learning.

The stability of this internally contradictory, adaptive and con-
tinually changing system is helped by the existence of 'organisational
slack'. This consists of payments to members of the coalition in excess
of what is required to maintain the organisation. It arises because of
frictions or imperfections in the mutual adjustment of payments and
demands so that there is ordinarily a disparity between the resources
available to the organisation and the payments required to maintain
the coalition. Since aspiration-level adjustment to achievement is a
relatively slow process – especially downward adjustment – then if the
only adaptive devices available were adjustments in aspirations of
members of the coalition, the system would be unstable in the face of
fluctuations in the environment. Organisational slack tends to stabilise
the system in two ways. First, by absorbing excess resources it retards
upward adjustment of aspirations during relatively good times. Second, by providing a pool of emergency resources it permits
aspirations to be maintained during relatively bad times.

Cyert and March conclude that conflict is never fully resolved
within an organisation. The decentralisation of decision-making, the

sequential attention to goals and the adjustment in organisational slack permit the business firm to make decisions with inconsistent goals under many conditions.

Managerial theories therefore contrast completely with the organisational approach. They focus on the top management group whose scope in pursuing its own goals clearly depends on the failure of other groups simultaneously to optimise with respect to their goals: typically, as with Williamson's and Baumol's minimum acceptable profit, it is assumed that managers maximise while owners satisfice. This assumption is justified by the empirical evidence presented, by the strategic position occupied by top management in the selection of goals, and by the greater clarity of the model which is achieved by viewing a firm as operated by one group – constrained by pressures from the rest – rather than as a permanent but ever-shifting coalition in which no single group is predominant.

There is in fact less difficulty in fitting profit maximisation into the organisational framework, since it represents a limiting case in which organisational slack is zero. O. E. Williamson has suggested[3] that organisational behaviour displays 'syndrome properties': either the organisation is run as a 'tight ship' or it is permitted to run slack. Intermediate positions are difficult to sustain because lower-level compliance is conditional upon higher-level example. The stance adopted by top management tends to characterise the whole operation and, as the condition of the environment deteriorates, this stance changes from slack to no-slack. Thus as the environment becomes less bountiful, internal conflicts between groups may at first increase, causing performance to suffer;[4] but the incentive to consensus will be overwhelming ultimately, leading to a stance indistinguishable from profit maximising.

Behavioural theory can be framed in a sufficiently precise manner to enable it to yield predictions. Its strength (or its weakness, depending on the use to which the model is to be put) is that different firms will respond in a different way to the same sets of circumstances. Thus, in contrast to the generality of traditional theory (or at least of the claims of traditional theory), it would try to forecast the behaviour of a particular organisation by discovering its goals, the order of priority of these goals, and its decision-making process. Cyert and March have used a simplified model allowing for three goals, three decisions per time period, an initial environment, aspiration levels which are modified in the light of experience, and organisational slack.

They have also used a simulation process to explore the behaviour of the organisation over 10,000 periods.

There is no point, having emphasised the differences between this and the traditional approach, in debating at length whether rule-of-thumb decision-making is irrational and whether behavioural models can be invested with sufficient generality to be accorded the distinction of being classified as a theory of the firm rather than a collection of interesting economic jigsaw puzzles. Each type of approach is suitable in the right context; both are capable of yielding insights useful to the other; and both have a great deal further to go. For instance, an example of the possible macroeconomic implications of the behavioural model is given in the Marris and Wood symposium *The Corporate Economy.*[5] Expansionary macroeconomic policies which shift the firm's demand curve to the right may lead to greater increases in output and employment and smaller increases in price if the firm's behavioural rule is simple capacity utilisation than if it operates as a traditional oligopolist. This is admitted to be 'rather speculative analysis'. To anyone predisposed to a neoclassical approach, the suggested behaviour appears neither surprising nor at odds with that approach. Models which specifically start with empirically based decision rules may cause questions to be raised which traditional analysis would not have asked but which it is quite capable of answering.

Perhaps one of the most important developments to emerge in this way is the emphasis which behavioural theory places on cost reduction, whereas the assumption in conventional models is that, for a given output, the least-cost combination of inputs has already been achieved. The term 'inefficiency' tends to have for the economist the connotation of an output other than that at which average cost is minimised; given the output, it is assumed that the constraint provided by the production function and the input prices (see below, p. 38) will be effective so that total cost is minimised. To the businessman, inefficiency has the connotation 'organisational slack at all outputs'. This distinction between allocative and internal efficiency is made by Leibenstein, who has coined the term 'X-efficiency' for the latter type:

> The data suggest that in a great many instances the amount to be gained by increased allocative efficiency is trivial while the amount to be gained by increasing X-efficiency is frequently significant.[6]

The point is that in this way efficiency is highlighted as a management preoccupation and resources have to be devoted to means of improving it. For example, if, to use the economist's term, profits greater than normal are being earned by a firm, the labour force will tend to seek goals such as leisure which are at variance with the profit goal, and the management will have to decide whether or not to devote policing resources (such as management consultants and work-study experts) in an effort to increase the X-efficiency of labour. Under competitive conditions it can be assumed that labour is forced to co-operate fully.[7]

The relationship between goals and X-efficiency is illustrated in Fig. 2.1.[8] In period t the output goal X_t has been achieved at average cost

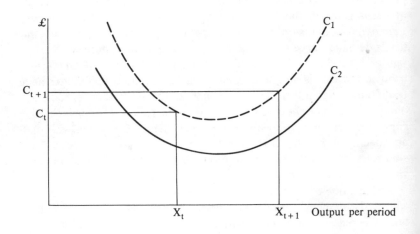

Output per period
Fig. 2.1

C_t, which at price P satisfies the profit goal π_t. In the next period the profit goal is $\pi_{t+1} > \pi_t$ and the output goal $X_{t+1} > X_t$ (assuming the firm desires both profit and output to grow). However, X_{t+1} at an average cost of C_{t+1} and unchanged P will not, except by pure chance, yield exactly π_{t+1}. If it yields less, the firm will institute a search routine which may produce a new estimate of average cost C_2 and profits satisfying the goal. The firm will not necessarily tend to discover the 'true' or lowest-cost curve, since it is subject to the counter-pressure of increasing X-inefficiency as a result of continued attainment of goals and a relaxation of the motivation to be as efficient as possible.

For the present, because of its emphasis on the inconsistency of goals and on the unresolved conflict in organisations, organisation theory will be allowed to form part of the background rather than the foreground of the theory of the firm.

NOTES AND REFERENCES

1. R. M. Cyert and J. G. March, *A Behavioral Theory of the Firm* (Englewood Cliffs, N.J.: Prentice-Hall, 1963)

2. Ibid., p. 30.

3. O. E. Williamson, 'A Dynamic Stochastic Theory of Managerial Behavior', in Phillips and Williamson (eds.), *Prices: Issues in Theory, Practice and Public Policy.*

4. See A. Phillips, 'An Attempt to Synthesise Some Theories of the Firm', ibid.

5. W. J. Baumol and M. Stewart, 'On the Behavioral Theory of the Firm', in Marris and Wood (eds.), *The Corporate Economy,* p. 140.

6. H. Leibenstein, 'Allocative Efficiency versus X-Efficiency', *American Economic Review* (June 1966) p. 413.

7. C. K. Rowley and M. A. Crew, 'Anti-Trust Policy: Economics versus Management Science', *Moorgate and Wall Street* (autumn 1970). Reprinted in C. K. Rowley (ed.) *Readings in Industrial Economics Vol. 2* (London: Macmillan 1972).

8. R. M. Cyert and K. D. George, 'Competition, Growth and Efficiency', *Economic Journal* (March 1969).

3

A PERSPECTIVE ON MANAGERIAL THEORIES

THE models which are considered here are optimisation models. In all of them a function is maximised with or without constraints: in this respect they are in the classical tradition. Non-maximising models may offer useful insights but they will be ultimately unsatisfactory if they fail to yield identifiable equilibrium conditions. Satisficing, mark-up pricing, adaptive systems, all run the risk of being no more than descriptions of business behaviour masquerading as economic analysis. Realism may in the end be destructive of logic and of understanding alike.

The models fall into two groups: static and dynamic. Comparative statics is defined by Samuelson as 'the investigation of changes in a system from one position of equilibrium to another without regard to the transitional process involved in the adjustment'.[1] This characterisation for the most part fits the present purpose, although it is normally permitted, even in comparative statics, to make some attempt to investigate the transitional processes. In the second part of the present chapter the outlines of classical and neoclassical static profit-maximisation theory are sketched, for it is necessary to define the traditional reference point from which managerial 'divergences' may be judged. In spite of managerialist aspirations to the contrary, there are logical as well as historical reasons for placing profit maximisation downstage. It will, however, be assumed that the reader is familiar, from basic microeconomics texts, with the details of profit-maximising models.

The static managerial models are those of W. J. Baumol and O. E. Williamson, which are discussed in Chapters 4 and 5 respectively. Both suggest that while profit is important (and it would be absurd to suggest otherwise in any context) the people who make decisions in large corporations are unlikely to be motivated to maximise it. Alternative maximands are introduced which pay attention to managerial psychology, and in both cases outlays on sales promotion are emphasised. There are differences in formulation and treatment. Williamson is more mathematical and also more general in the sense that the objective function is managerial utility, which in principle could have any number of elements and in fact has three. Baumol neatly offers a single proxy variable for managerial aspirations – sales revenue. A significant difference is that whereas Baumol managers want to make profit only in so far as this is consistent with increasing sales or in so far as they are forced to do so by shareholders, Williamson managers have a positive desire for profit, which nevertheless competes with their desire for income and status as reflected in expenditure on staff or on perquisites. The Baumol model has provoked a great deal of comment and some of this is also discussed in Chapter 4.

The models in the second group are not static but, on the other hand, the adjective 'dynamic' would require some justification. It is a matter of discovering an authoritative definition which will fit the characteristics of the models we wish to include. Samuelson's definition of dynamics would involve 'functional equations in which variables at different points of time are involved in an essential way' – which would not be appropriate. Hicks puts it as follows:

> In mechanics, statics is concerned with rest, dynamics with motion; but no economic system is ever at rest in anything like the mechanical sense. Production is itself a process; by its very nature it is a process of change. All we can do is to define a static condition as one in which certain key variables are unchanging. A dynamic condition is then one in which they are changing. And dynamic theory is the analysis of the processes by which they change.[2]

The key variables of the static theory of the firm are prices of inputs and outputs, quantities of inputs and outputs per time period and, in some cases, outlay on marketing per time period. The key variables of the dynamic theory of the firm are rates of change. It is worth noting, however, that although in the dynamic theory we look at, for example, the rate of change, over time, of output per period (rather than the level of output per period), in fact so-called steady-state growth implies no change (in equilibrium) in the established rates of change (growth rates). Marris considers his approach to be comparative dynamics: the equilibrium conditions having been deduced from the characteristics of the model, the effect of changes in exogenous variables is considered. Samuelson's transitional process is ignored almost completely:

> As a matter of fact there is a sense in which the theory could be translated into comparative statics, although one might reasonably think that where at least one of the main objective variables is a rate of change, to do so would be stretching the language unduly.[3]

Growth theory is considered in Chapters 6 and 7. Baumol's contribution in this field, in his 1962 article,[4] was to use the idea of discounting the firm's profits over time, and to distinguish between profit before and after the costs of the growth process had been deducted. J. H. Williamson's 1966 article[5] was a significant step forward, which made possible much of the succeeding work by other writers. He formalised the mathematics, separated out expansion costs more specifically than Baumol had done, and showed how different managerial objectives would lead to different policies for static variables such as output as well as for dynamic ones such as dividend and growth rate. He also formally incorporated a take-over threat as the chief constraint on the growth policies of managers. Chapter 6 is based essentially on the ideas of Baumol and J. H. Williamson. However, in some cases their treatment has either turned out to be misleading or has been replaced by a simpler method of arriving at the same result. Marris's characteristic contribution in *Managerial Capitalism,* which takes up Chapter 7, is partly in the theory of valuation – the relationship between the growth of the firm and its market value; partly in the formulation of a managerial utility function with growth as a major element; partly in the theory of demand – the idea that by incurring expenditure on research and diversification, markets can be created; and ultimately in the formulation of a model in which take-over is the ultimate constraint. Much of the earlier work in growth theory is tidied up, and the theory advanced several stages, in *The Corporate Economy,* edited by Marris and Wood.

There is a sense, of course, in which all 'theory of the firm' leads inexorably towards managerial theory, and all managerial theory towards growth theory – with the implication that in the context of corporate capitalism the only theory worth looking at is a dynamic managerial theory. Certainly such a theory is extremely general since it includes, as special cases, zero managerial discretion and zero growth. But it is still not universally accepted that growth is or should be the primary objective of either the corporation or the economy as a whole; and even if it were, there would be a place for the static or non-managerial models for use in situations where their assumptions were suitable, and therefore their greater capacity to focus on detail was an advantage. In principle, traditional microeconomics could have had a theory of the growth of the firm, as well as an explanation of the relationship between market value and product-market performance, an account of the diversification process and a theory of merger. In fact, for the most part, it failed to provide them, partly because it viewed the nature of capitalism as essentially a competitive, resource-allocating system with no discretion for the atoms of which it was constituted. Admittedly the system had generated a few harmful mutations, but it was for the most part well behaved, principally through the twin agencies of perfect information and managerial diseconomies of scale (U-shaped long-run average cost). The L-shaped long-run average-cost curve has given non-owning managers their discretionary power, because through the joint-stock company they control the large investment in capital equipment which is required to achieve the minimum efficient scale of operations. It has also given rise to the economist's search for the diseconomies of growth which would yield a determinate equilibrium for the growth rate of the firm, where unexhausted economies of scale might leave its size indeterminate. 'Might' — because, as elementary monopoly theory demonstrates, the falling demand curve for a product may put a limit to the size of the firm even though as a productive organisation it is capable of turning out a bigger output at lower unit cost. A theory of growth thus emerges out of the need to explain why a firm with L-shaped average cost could not expand indefinitely by taking output of a given product up to the limit mentioned above and then adding a further product to its mix.

The rest of this chapter is given over to a summary of the results of classical and neoclassical theory for the purpose of comparison with the managerial models which follow.

COMPETITIVE MODEL

A profit-maximising model of the firm will probably be appropriate to situations where the firm buys its inputs and sells its outputs in competitive markets. The purpose of such a model is not to simulate the decision process in the individual firm but to predict the aggregate or market response to parameter changes. Since Marshall, attention has been focused on an abstraction in order to 'discover the causes which govern the supply price of a commodity'. This abstraction is the 'representative firm',

> which has had a fairly long life and fair success, which is managed with normal ability and which has normal access to the economies, external and internal, which belong to that aggregate volume of production.[6]

The firm, then, is the resource-allocating unit. The problems arising from considering the firm as an administrative and social organisation are not relevant. (Except that, since technical economies of scale are widespread, the argument has to be that it is organisational diseconomies that render the scale of operations determinate.) Profit maximisation in such circumstances is not so much a behavioural assumption as a necessary condition for survival, given that the system is made up of individuals who, whether producing or consuming, are knowledgeable in their single-minded pursuit of maximum 'profit'.

Since marginal cost equals price (see Appendix, pp. 38–40 below), maximum social benefit is obtained: the opportunity cost in scarce resources of the marginal unit produced just balances the benefit derived by the (utility-maximising) consumer who buys it. Since average cost is minimised (the model assumes there is an optimum scale) the firm is at its most efficient, in the allocative as well as the Leibenstein sense, and has no excess capacity. In the long run, price equals average cost: any tendency of profits to rise above opportunity-cost returns in a particular sector will attract resources from other sectors; if there are no market imperfections preventing or distorting resource flows, rent elements will disappear from the system.

Comparative Static Responses for Competitive Model

(a) An increase in demand emerges as an increase in market price. The output of the firm and of the industry increase in the short run; in the long run the output of the firm is unchanged but the number of firms increases. Long-run market price is unchanged.

(b) A sales tax shifts marginal cost upwards, reduces output of both firm and industry and raises market price by less than the amount of the tax in the short run but by the full amount of the tax in the long run.

(c) A profits tax has no effect on output or price.

(d) A lump-sum tax or increase in fixed cost has no effect in the short run. In the long run the output of sufficient firms will go to zero to enable the remainder to maintain normal profit. Long-run market price will be higher and output lower. The output of the individual firm which remains will be less than before because higher relative prices of short-run fixed resources, compared with variable resources, reduce the optimum scale of plant.[7]

MONOPOLY

This is perhaps the most relevant starting-point for a consideration of managerial theories because the model is consistent with profits above survival level and therefore allows for managerial discretion. It also provides a convenient theoretical framework for overtly managerial models to build on – for example, the Baumol model. The equilibrium conditions for monopoly are different from those of competition, differences which are significant from the welfare point of view. Because the monopolist faces a demand which is a decreasing function of price, in equilibrium price will be above marginal cost: resources are under-allocated to the industry, the output is too small and the price too high. Because entry is difficult price is probably above average cost and too much profit is made. Average cost will not be minimised, except by chance.

Comparative Static Responses for Monopoly

These are similar to those of a competitive firm, the main differences being the greater ambiguity of response to increases in demand.

(a) An increase in demand may lead either to an increase or to a decrease in price depending on whether unit cost is rising or falling and on the elasticity of demand. Fig. 3.1 shows price falling. As demand increases from D_1 to D_2, marginal revenue shifts from M_1 to M_2. Price falls from P_1 to P_2.

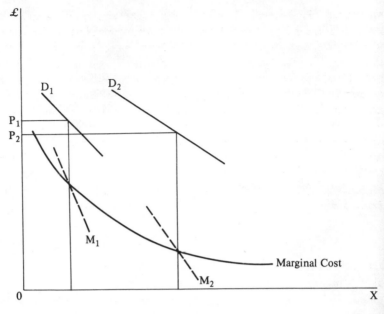

Fig. 3.1

(b) Taxes elicit the same response as from the competitive firm, but because of the identity of the firm and industry they are if anything easier to handle. For example, the rise in price after a sales tax will always be less than the amount of the tax.

The prediction that the firm will maintain price and output unaltered in the short run in the face of lump-sum or profit taxes has been an important source of dissatisfaction in view of the frequently observed tendency of firms in practice to raise prices to cover rises in fixed costs.

OLIGOPOLY

Managerial theories are almost exclusively theories of oligopoly since they are about large firms who are competing, for the most part, with a few others. The problem with oligopoly, of course, is that before deciding on appropriate strategies the decision-maker must take account of rivals' potential responses – the problem of 'conjectural variations'. This means applying either the theory of games or possibly some other approach (e.g. a Cournot-type model). Economy of effort has usually meant that if the interdependence of rivals were the aspect of the situation to be emphasised, the complexity of managerial motives would be ignored and simple profit maximisation assumed. Similarly, if the main objective is to emphasise managerial goals there tend to be sufficient complications without the extra ones which interdependence would bring. Thus, for example, Baumol's sales-maximising model explicitly ignores interdependence. On the other hand, managerial models are in principle adaptable to deal with conjectural variations, as has been demonstrated by Marris in both *Managerial Capitalism* (see Chapter 7 below) and *The Corporate Economy*.

MONOPOLISTIC COMPETITION

This model is worth mentioning for two reasons:

1. It represents the limiting monopoly case where monopoly profit is zero, but resource misallocation remains, as can be seen from Fig. 3.2, since price is greater than marginal cost and optimum size is not reached. The exercise of managerial discretion is impossible.

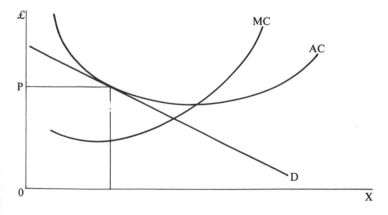

Fig. 3.2

2. It is a neoclassical example of a tendency observable to a marked degree in managerial models. This is the tendency for the determinacy of the model to decrease at an increasing rate as the number of decision variables is increased while the model is kept at a high level of generality.

For example, if a sales tax is imposed it is not possible to predict whether price rises or not, when allowance has to be made for ensuing changes in the quality of the product and in the level of advertising, as well as in output, given only the general characteristics of the model (differentiated products, free entry and profit maximisation). Precise functional relationships would have to be specified for determinacy to be achieved.[8] On the other hand, monopolistic competition belies the assumption that neoclassical theory is restricted to price/output decisions and that the introduction of other variables was a discovery of managerial theory.

Historically, managerial theories may be seen as an extension or an expansion of entrepreneurial models such as those described in this chapter. Logically, however, it becomes apparent that managerial models are more general and include entrepreneurial models as special cases where certain variables become insignificant or vanish. The dichotomy between generality and determinacy is well known. Yet no matter how realistic, particular and completely specified the model at the outset, there is an irresistible temptation to try for a more general applicability. This applies to Baumol and Marris as much as to Chamberlin.[9]

APPENDIX: PROFIT-MAXIMISING EQUILIBRIUM

The competitive model may be generalised as follows for a production process with k inputs and m outputs. The production function is

$$f(X_1, X_2, \ldots, X_n) = 0 \qquad (3.1)$$

where $X_i > 0$ is the quantity of the ith output and $X_i < 0$ the quantity of the ith input and where $k + m = n$.

Given the prices (P_i) of inputs and outputs the problem is to choose X_i so as to maximise profit:

$$\pi = \sum_{i=1}^{n} X_i P_i \qquad (3.2)$$

subject to (3.1). The first-order conditions for a maximum are obtained from the Lagrangean function

$$Z = \pi - \lambda f.$$

The conditions are

$$P_i = \lambda f_i$$
$$f = 0. \qquad (3.3)$$

The ratio f_i/f_j is the rate of technical substitution between the ith and jth inputs or outputs and, by (3.3), efficient resource use requires

$$\frac{f_i}{f_j} = \frac{P_i}{P_j}$$

i.e. the rate of substitution within the firm must be equal to the rate of exchange in the market place. The second-order condition for maximum profit is

$$d^2 Z < 0.$$

But

$$d^2 Z = -\lambda d^2 f$$

and since, by assumption, $\lambda > 0$, we require

$$d^2 f > 0.$$

By the theory of quadratic forms[10] this requires all the relevant bordered Hessians to be negative — a condition equivalent to the assumption that the production surface is convex at the stationary point.

In the particular case of a firm producing a single product X, cost and revenue can be reduced to functions of X so that profit becomes

$$\pi = \pi(X) = R(X) - C(X)$$

where R is total revenue and C total cost. This yields the first-order condition

$$\frac{dR}{dX} = \frac{dC}{dX} \qquad (3.4)$$

which is in general true for all profit maximisers and which (since

$dR/dX = dPX/dX = P + XdP/dX)$ reduces, for the competitive firm, to

$$P = \frac{dC}{dX} \qquad (3.5)$$

because, being a price-taker, $dP/dX = 0$. The firm thus sets marginal cost equal to price. The second-order condition is

$$\frac{d^2R}{dX^2} < \frac{d^2C}{dX^2}. \qquad (3.6)$$

For the competitive firm $d^2R/dX^2 = 0$ (price is unaffected by the size of output), so that the condition reduces to

$$\frac{d^2C}{dX^2} > 0 \qquad (3.7)$$

that is, marginal cost must be rising in perfect competition while in the general case the second-order condition is that marginal cost cut marginal revenue from below.[11]

The economic assumptions of the model also involve the implicit inclusion of a further constraint in addition to (3.1):

$$\pi = 0 \qquad (3.8)$$

through long-run adjustment of the P_i In the short run we may have $\pi \gtrless 0$.

In the case of monopoly (3.8) ceases to hold and becomes $\pi \geqslant 0$. The first-order condition (3.4) still applies, but since for the monopolist $dP/dX < 0$, we have (compared with (3.5)) $P > dC/dX$. The second-order condition is still (3.6), but since $d^2R/dX^2 < 0$ the highly significant (3.7) no longer applies. As long as marginal cost is flatter than marginal revenue at their intersection (as in Fig. 3.1), the size of the firm will be determinate.

NOTES AND REFERENCES

1. P. A. Samuelson, *Foundations of Economic Analysis* (Cambridge, Mass.: Harvard Univ. Press, 1963).
2. J. R. Hicks, *Capital and Growth* (Oxford Univ. Press, 1965) p. 6.
3. *Managerial Capitalism*, p. 127.

4. W. J. Baumol, 'On the Theory of Expansion of the Firm', *American Economic Review* (Dec. 1962). Reprinted in G. C. Archibald (ed.) *The Theory of the Firm*, (Harmondsworth: Penguin Books 1971).

5. J. H. Williamson, 'Profit, Growth and Sales Maximisation', *Economica* (Feb. 1966). Reprinted in G. C. Archibald op. cit. and in D. Needham (ed.) *Readings in the Economics of Industrial Organisation* (New York: Holt, Rinehart & Winston 1970).

6. A. Marshall, *Principles of Economics,* 8th ed. (London: Macmillan, 1920) p. 317.

7. See, for example, R. H. Leftwich, *The Price System and Resource Allocation,* 4th ed. (New York: Holt, Rinehart & Winston, 1970) chap. 9.

8. G. C. Archibald demonstrates this rigorously in 'The Comparative Statics of Monopolistic Competition', in G. C. Archibald (ed.), *The Theory of the Firm* (Harmondsworth: Penguin Books, 1971).

9. E. H. Chamberlin, *The Theory of Monopolistic Competition* (Oxford Univ. Press, 1933).

10. R. G. D. Allen, *Mathematical Analysis for Economists* (London: Macmillan, 1938) p. 485; also J. M. Henderson and R. E. Quandt, *Microeconomic Theory* 2nd edition (New York: McGraw-Hill, 1971) pp. 401–7.

11. This conclusion places a constraint upon the nature of the production function (3.1). In particular, linear homogeneous production functions will not be appropriate to perfect competition, since with constant input prices they yield constant marginal cost.

4

REVENUE MAXIMISATION

THE problem of oligopolistic interdependence was mentioned in the last chapter as one which managerial models may in principle cope with but may prefer to avoid. Baumol[1] asserts that in day-to-day decision-making conjectural variation plays a small role, for three reasons:

1. The complexity of internal organisation which makes decision-making a lengthy and unpredictable process.
2. The use of rules of thumb instead of optimising techniques because top executives are too busy and their computational skills too limited. Simple and widely understood rules of thumb minimise the danger of behaviour intended to be peaceful and co-operative being misunderstood as predatory or retaliatory.
3. Desire for a quiet life: the pursuit of goals such as respectability and security; unwillingness to incur the disapproval of public authorities; the existence of a code of professional conduct or etiquette.

The assertion in general hardly seems valid. No one suggests that day-to-day decisions would take interdependence into account. It is in the areas of major policy on investment, pricing and advertising, which are important to the Baumol model, that by his own admission a game-theory approach would be more appropriate. However, in this model, as in all those which follow, the approach is deterministic rather than probabilistic.

BASIC MODEL

Baumol presents his model as typical of oligopolistic behaviour, although he is well aware of the dangers of over-generalisation. The objective is sales maximisation subject to a minimum profit constraint. Profit maximisation is rejected because it leaves unexplained some features of oligopolistic behaviour such as the tendency to raise price to cover increases in fixed costs. Scale (and thus sales revenue) is an important proximate objective to profit since large size increases the magnitude of the funds which can be accumulated to finance further expansion. (It is certainly worth noting that, over large ranges of output, revenue and profit will increase together; though attention is naturally concentrated upon situations where these goals conflict.) Size of course implies several other things which managers might find equally desirable, such as security and prestige. And managerial salaries may be related more to sales than to profits.

The minimum profit level is seen as a constraint imposed by the capital market and by the need to pay owners a return comparable to that paid by others. It is defined as that level of profit which just satisfies shareholders when divided between dividends and reinvestment in a manner which most clearly accords with their preferences. Of course, if product- and capital-market conditions were competitive, the minimum acceptable profit would be maximum profit. This would leave all participants with opportunity-cost returns and prevent management from pursuing a separate sales goal. The successful achievement of such a goal at the expense of profit implies monopolistic product markets where abnormal profit is earned to which investors in an imperfect capital market are unable to lay claim.

Of course it is not just the level of profit but also the retention policy which determines shareholder acquiescence. Baumol's loose rationalisation of minimum profit is as follows:

> In practice minimum acceptable profit is a rough attempt to provide completely acceptable earnings to stockholders while leaving enough over for investment in future output expansion at the maximum rate which management considers to be reasonably safely marketable.[2]

Thus in single-period analysis we shall to some extent gloss over the perfectly valid criticism of the static model that the minimum profit level is not specifically determined.[3] We shall rely on the intuitively reasonable nature of the concept and leave the problems to be ironed out in the multi-period models which follow.

The model can be formulated as follows:

$$\text{maximise} \quad R = R(X, S) \tag{4.1}$$
$$\text{subject to} \quad \pi \geqslant \pi_0 \tag{4.2}$$
$$X, S \geqslant 0 \tag{4.3}$$

where $R = PX$ = total revenue or sales

X = output

S = expenditure on staff which in this context means general outlay on sales promotion or advertising

$\pi = (1 - t)(R - C - S - \bar{T})$ = profit

$C = C(X)$ = total production cost

t = profit-tax rate

$\bar{T}$ = any lump-sum tax

π_0 = minimum acceptable profit.

Note that sales are a function of advertising and of output, which is itself a function (demand curve) of price. Total cost is $(C - S - \bar{T})$ and pre-tax profit is $(R - C - S - \bar{T})$. With a profit-tax rate of t, post-tax profit is

$$\pi = (1 - t)(R - C - S - \bar{T}).$$

The equilibrium conditions of the model are obtained by forming the Lagrangean function

$$Z(X, S, \lambda) = R - \lambda(\pi - \pi_0).$$

The Kuhn–Tucker conditions[4] for maximum R require

$$\frac{\partial Z}{\partial X} \leqslant 0, \qquad \frac{\partial Z}{\partial S} \leqslant 0, \qquad \frac{\partial Z}{\partial \lambda} \geqslant 0. \qquad (4.4)$$

where the latter expression is equivalent to (4.2). Differentiating first with respect to X,

$$\frac{\partial Z}{\partial X} = \frac{\partial R}{\partial X} - \lambda(1 - t)\left(\frac{\partial R}{\partial X} - \frac{\partial C}{\partial X}\right) \leqslant 0. \qquad (4.5)$$

Assume Z is a concave function which takes on its maximum where $X > 0$. That is, assume the revenue and cost functions have their usual characteristics and that condition (3.6) holds. Then if $X > 0$ (the firm produces at all), the first-order condition becomes[5] $\partial Z/\partial X = 0$. From (4.5), then, we have

$$\lambda(1 - t)\frac{\partial R}{\partial X} - \frac{\partial R}{\partial X} = \lambda(1 - t)\frac{\partial C}{\partial X}$$

so that

$$\frac{\partial R}{\partial X} = \frac{\lambda(1 - t)}{\lambda(1 - t) - 1}\frac{\partial C}{\partial X}. \qquad (4.6)$$

Since $t < 1$, the relationship between marginal revenue and marginal cost depends on whether $\lambda < 0$ or $\lambda = 0$. This in turn depends on whether the constraint (4.2) is effective or not.

(a) If $\pi > \pi_0$ the constraint is not effective (places no restriction on behaviour in the equilibrium situation) and $\lambda = 0$.[6] Then, from (4.5),

$$\frac{\partial R}{\partial X} = 0$$

a solution which is illustrated in Fig. 4.1. X_R is the revenue-maximising output where elasticity of demand is unity, X_M the profit-maximising monopolist's output. Profit at X_R is more than the minimum required.

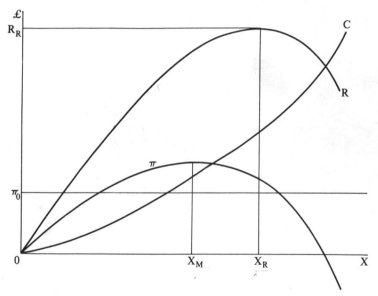

FIG. 4.1

(b) If $\pi = \pi_0$ the constraint is effective and $\lambda < 0$. From (4.6) the equilibrium condition is

$$\frac{\partial R}{\partial X} < \frac{\partial C}{\partial X} \, . \tag{4.7}$$

This is shown in Fig. 4.2, where the constrained maximum revenue is R_C at an output of X_C. Thus except for the limiting case where π_0 is such that $X_M = X_C$, the sales maximiser always produces more than the profit maximiser, taking output into the range where marginal production cost is greater than marginal revenue, reducing profit.

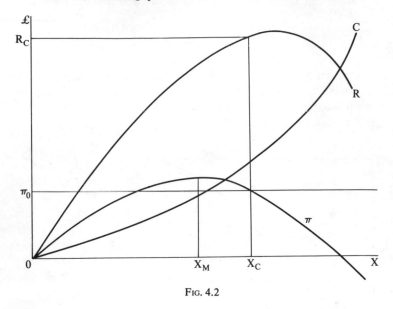

Fig. 4.2

Returning to (4.4) and differentiating Z this time with respect to S, we find

$$\frac{\partial Z}{\partial S} = \frac{\partial R}{\partial S} - \lambda(1-t)\frac{\partial R}{\partial S} + \lambda(1-t) \leqslant 0. \qquad (4.8)$$

(a) Following the same argument as before, with $\pi > \pi_0$ and $S > 0$ we have $\partial Z/\partial S = 0$, and $\lambda = 0$. Then, from (4.8),

$$\frac{\partial R}{\partial S} = 0.$$

Further advertising is incapable of persuading consumers either to pay a higher price for an existing quantity or to buy more at the same price. Taken with the solution shown in Fig. 4.1, this means the firm has sufficient margin of profit to push both advertising and output to the limit of their effectiveness in producing revenue.

(b) With $\pi = \pi_0$ and $S > 0$, $\partial Z/\partial S = 0$ and $\lambda < 0$. (4.8) yields

$$\frac{\partial R}{\partial S} = \frac{\lambda(1-t)}{\lambda(1-t)-1} < 1. \qquad (4.9)$$

This may be compared with the profit-maximising level of advertising by setting $\partial\pi/\partial S = 0$ to yield $\partial R/\partial S = 1$. The constrained sales maximiser, although not taking advertising to the limit of its effectiveness, will take it beyond the point where it brings in as much revenue as it costs.

It is obviously important to consider the likelihood of a type (b) outcome with non-maximised profit at the minimum acceptable level. A reduction in generality will greatly increase determinacy: if $\pi = \pi_0$, the equilibrium values of X and S can be chosen, from which R, C and P will be automatically determined, given the relevant functions. This is therefore preferable to $\pi \geqslant \pi_0$ on the grounds of the model's manageability.

The likelihood of having $\pi = \pi_0$ depends on the nature of $R(S)$. As it stands, we have the possibility of achieving $\partial R/\partial S = 0$ before profit has been reduced to π_0. The way out chosen by Baumol is plausible and justified and it consists in placing a restriction on the character of $R(S)$ by assuming that the marginal revenue of advertising is always positive:

$$\frac{\partial R}{\partial S} > 0. \qquad (4.10)$$

In other words, although advertising may become less and less effective it will always increase sales, even if only slightly. Then the profit constraint will always be effective; unneeded profit will be eroded by unprofitable advertising; the output will be X_C in Fig. 4.2 and will be greater than that of the profit maximiser; price ($P_C = R_C/X_C$) will be less.

The equilibrium level of advertising is shown in Fig. 4.3, where such outlay is given by a 45° line through the origin. Since production cost $[C(X)]$ is not a function of advertising, a fixed outlay on production is added to advertising cost to yield the linear total cost (TC). As Baumol admits, the assumption that non-advertising cost is independent of the level of advertising is virtually certain to be false, since if advertising increases sales it will presumably increase production and distribution cost. The implication of the diagram is that advertising is permitted to increase revenue only by allowing a rise in the price at which the given output is sold. There is of course no unconstrained maximum R. S_C is the constrained equilibrium level of advertising whereas the profit maximiser's level of advertising is S_M Sales maximisers advertise more than profit maximisers.

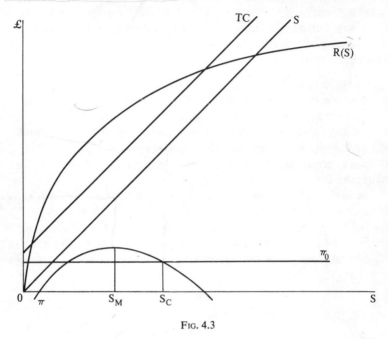

FIG. 4.3

ADVERTISING AND PRICE DECISIONS

Ambiguities in Baumol's treatment of price and advertising decisions are the basis of a criticism by R. L. Sandmeyer.[7] In explaining the nature of $R(S)$, Baumol had maintained that 'unlike a price reduction a *ceteris paribus* rise in advertising expenditure involves no change in the market value of the item sold'.[8] Apart from anything else, this obviously runs counter to the interpretation of Fig. 4.3 as allowing advertising to affect price but not volume. Furthermore, Sandmeyer suggests that, by assuming price to be given when the firm varies advertising outlay, Baumol does not consider the case where the firm changes price along with the advertising budget (both of which influence output) in order to obtain the highest sales given the minimum profit restriction. In other words, the $R(S)$ function of Fig. 4.3 assumes a fixed price (perhaps R_C/X_C from Fig. 4.2 or R_R/X_R from Fig. 4.1). Baumol has claimed that variation of price and advertising together is implicit in his own account. Whether this is the case or not is relatively unimportant: Sandmeyer's method makes the adjustment process explicit. It is illustrated in Fig. 4.4. The idea is that minimum profit can be treated as a fixed cost while advertising outlays increase through discrete increments, each of which generates a new revenue function. The lines $(C + \pi_0)$ shift upwards at a constant rate as extra units of advertising are introduced. For example, with advertising outlay at zero and production cost at C_0 the revenue function is R_0.

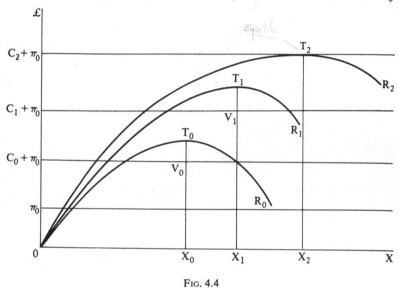

FIG. 4.4

Equilibrium output is X_0, revenue is maximised at T_0 and price is $T_0 X_0 / X_0$ yielding a surplus profit of $T_0 V_0$. The firm can increase revenue by increasing advertising and by changing price (in general there is no presumption that price will either rise consistently or fall consistently throughout the process). One unit of advertising yields total 'cost' $C_1 + \pi_0$ and revenue function R_1 with surplus profit $T_1 V_1$. This continues until equilibrium is reached with advertising outlay C_2, output X_2 and price $T_2 X_2 / X_2$.

Useful though this is, it carries the misleading implication that, in equilibrium, marginal revenue is zero and equal to marginal cost. It cannot therefore be called a generalisation of the model and is indeed inconsistent with the condition (4.7) and the solution at X_C in Fig. 4.2.

Haveman and DeBartolo[9] have adapted the Sandmeyer method so as to allow for non-zero marginal cost, as shown in Fig. 4.5. We begin from a Sandmeyer equilibrium at X_0 where total 'cost' ($\pi_0 + C + s$) equals revenue ($R(S = s)$). $S = s$ is the equilibrium level of advertising.

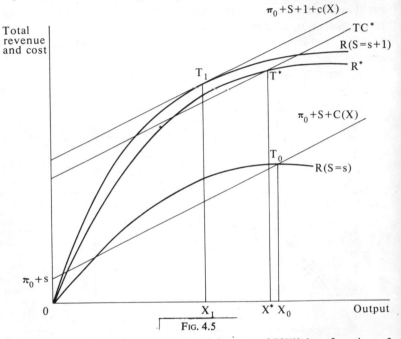

FIG. 4.5

In the Haveman version, non-advertising cost ($C(X)$) is a function of output, so that at T_0 total 'cost' would be $\pi_0 + s + C(X)$. Equilibrium has thus not been reached since revenue can be further increased by purchasing an extra quantity of advertising. A further series of adjustments of advertising and price thus takes place, each increment of advertising producing a new revenue function. The highest revenue function consistent with the profit constraint is that labelled $R(S = s + 1)$, which is tangent to the appropriate cost curve ($\pi_0 + s + 1 + C(X)$) at T_1. However, this cannot be the sales maximiser's equilibrium since at this point $\partial R/\partial X = \partial C/\partial X$, whereas the equilibrium condition (4.7) demands $\partial R/\partial X < \partial C/\partial X$. Equilibrium is found at T^* on R^*, with, compared to T_1, less advertising, greater output and lower price. The points T_0, T_1 and T^* all satisfy the condition $\pi = \pi_0$, but T^* is the overall maximum revenue. The logic of this solution has been clearly demonstrated by C. J. Hawkins.[10] He uses a two-dimensional indifference curve diagram to represent the three-dimensional surface which results when R is expressed as a function of both S and X. The result is shown in Fig. 4.6. The iso-cost lines show all points of equal outlay on various combinations of advertising and production cost. They are straight lines on the assumption that average production cost is constant. The iso-revenue curves show combinations of output and advertising which yield the same sales revenue, on the assumption that both activities are subject to diminishing returns in terms of revenue generation. The

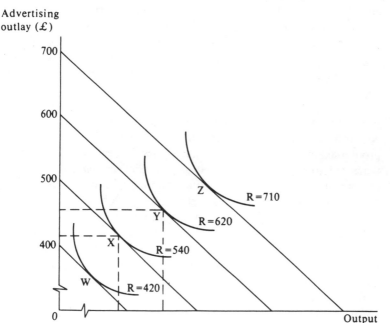

FIG. 4.6

equilibrium of the profit maximiser is at X, where the difference between revenue and cost is greatest. The sales maximiser will also choose a point of tangency, since for any given outlay he will want maximum revenue. If the minimum acceptable profit is £20, either W or Y could be chosen, but since Y yields greater revenue it will be preferred. An extremely important result follows from the Hawkins analysis: it is not necessarily true that sales maximisers produce more than profit maximisers, nor is it necessarily true that they advertise more. Although Fig. 4.6 shows an increase in both output and advertising between X and Y, it is quite clear that the tangencies W, X, Y and Z could be such as to render either advertising or output an 'inferior activity' whose level decreased in the search for greater revenue.

Whether or not something like Fig. 4.5 is implicit in Baumol's account, he cannot really avoid the charge that he has not given a convincing explanation of the price-setting process. This is particularly so since he himself stresses the point that the large firm has an independent and definite price policy. It is not merely that by implication he abandons price policy in favour of changing advertising budgets, but that throughout he presents the firm as an output-fixer rather than a price-fixer. Analysis of the pricing process actually occurring in oligopolistic firms would in general tend to lead in the direction of full-cost theories or variants on them, which Baumol regards as at best yielding a rough approximation to his own.

The use of a rule-of-thumb procedure for determining price may be justified in many ways. Indeed the attempts of people to justify full-cost behaviour by reference to some other yardstick – whether it be profit maximising or not – have caused much resentment. A full-coster tends not to relish being treated as a maximiser *manqué*. However, one might risk the suggestion that ignorance of marginal cost and marginal revenue may have something to do with it; that the cost of making the optimal decision may exceed the rise in profit; that the difficulty of choosing an optimal price strategy may cause unacceptable demands to be made upon managerial time; or finally, and perhaps most hurtfully for full-costers, that the shape of the unit-cost curve may be such that full costing is profit maximising with a different vocabulary!

Fig. 4.7 shows a profit-maximising output of X_M and price P, with average variable cost, and therefore marginal cost, constant over normal ranges of output. The full-cost method of determining price and output would be as follows:

1. Set price by costing up:
    (*a*) Take direct cost per unit (average variable cost).
    (*b*) Add unit overheads (average fixed cost).
    (*c*) Add a net profit margin.
2. Sell as much as possible at this price.

The procedure leaves unanswered many questions which the well-brought-up optimiser is bursting to ask. How can unit costs be determined until output is known? What happens if demand increases and output is greater than X_0? But of course a rule of thumb is meant for normal circumstances and cannot be expected to have an internal logic which makes it valid for all situations (nor, to be fair to critics of full cost, should its advocates feel they must claim consistency for it).

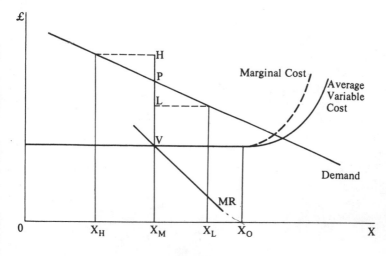

Fig. 4.7

One of the more interesting questions concerns what Andrews called the costing margin: 'The costing margin will normally tend to cover the costs of the indirect factors of production and provide a normal level of net profit, looking at the industry as a whole.'[11] The obvious ambiguity, again to anyone expecting a model to display some kind of internal consistency, lies in the nature of the profit margin. To shorten a protracted debate, if the profit margin is genuinely set by rule – say a fixed percentage – it will not yield maximum profit except by chance. If the margin is flexible and susceptible to market influences, as the quotation from Andrews suggests, we have not a rule of thumb but marginalist calculations by a different name.

The inflexible rule could be rational, of course, if it served objectives other than profit. In Figure 4.7, for example, a full-coster, assuming that normal output would be less than X_0, would not, except by chance, add a costing margin of VP. He might add more (say VH) or less (say *VL*). Managers who tended to add a bigger margin and sell less than the profit-maximising output might be aiming for a smaller work-load deliberately. Those who tended to add a smaller margin might be pursuing, albeit less precisely, the same objects as the sales maximiser. This brings us back to Baumol.

Baumol's attempt[12] to contrast full-cost pricing and maximising sales is illustrated in Fig. 4.8. The curve π_u is the minimum acceptable

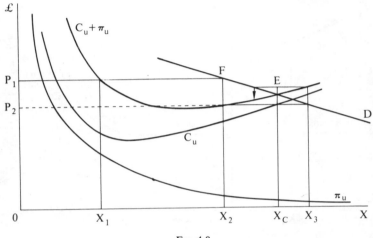

Fig. 4.8

profit per unit, C_u is the total cost per unit and $C_u + \pi_u$ is obtained by vertical summation. *D* is the demand curve. The assumption is that the sales maximiser is aware of the relevant demand and cost functions and can therefore successfully optimise, whereas the full-cost firm, being ignorant of the functions, must (as we have seen) achieve its second-rate salvation by trial and error through the application of a mark-up rule. The equilibrium for the sales maximiser will be at *E* at an output of X_C: demand is relatively elastic at this point and so marginal revenue is positive; if demand were inelastic, output would be reduced and price raised to increase revenue; if it were of unit elasticity, the adjustment process described would take place. Advertising outlay would increase, the $C_u + \pi_u$ curve and the *D* curve would shift upwards, and equilibrium would be achieved at a point such as *E* where the demand is relatively elastic.

Baumol claims that *E* is also the full-cost solution and is concerned mainly to expose the deficiencies of the process by which it is achieved, when compared with his own. It is not clear to him exactly how a mark-up system would arrive at a price where the output were such that the required level of unit profit were achieved. If the initial expected output were X_1 on the basis, say, of an inaccurate market survey, the full-cost price would be P_1. But at this price, actual output sold will be X_2 and profits will be greater than expected. Price is then lowered to P_2, output increases to X_3, and E is eventually reached along the path shown by the arrowed line.

Even if this sequence were a realistic account of how a full-cost price were achieved, it is not certain that it would result in equilibrium at E at all, since if the $C_u + \pi_u$ curve has a steeper slope than the D curve, the sequence of full-cost prices will move further and further away from equilibrium.

There are several unsatisfactory features of this description:

1. If full-cost is an attempt to secure a satisfactory profit with the minimum of decision-making cost, the Baumol sequence of advertising outlays shifting both $C_u + \pi_u$ and D upwards will not necessarily take place, so that equilibrium would occur on a different demand curve at a point where elasticity could be greater than, equal to or less than unity.

2. The cost curves of Fig. 4.8 would not be the basis for rational full-cost pricing, which is most appropriate where the average variable cost is flat over a wide range of output and where average fixed cost is so low as to be legitimately assumed constant. Thus, for example, at F the position is that the firm has by setting the price P_1 achieved a greater output than anticipated: cost per unit is lower and both profit margin and aggregate profit are greater. There is no justification for the rigid application of rule of thumb in these circumstances and one could reasonably expect the firm to maintain the price P_1.

3. The full-cost rule is to add on a fixed profit margin: this will yield aggregate profit proportionate to the quantity sold. This is not properly shown by the curve π_u, which is obtained by assuming a total profit constraint to be met and implying that the profit margin should diminish as output increases.

It is quite clear, then, that full-cost pricing is not at all the same thing as revenue maximising. To that extent Baumol is justified. On the other hand, the Baumol model is itself basically devoid of pricing implications. As in all optimising models, the optimal values of the decision variables emerge in solution: they are not chosen according to any operational rule. That is the reason why full cost cannot be reconciled with either revenue maximising or profit maximising and why the attempt to do so is fundamentally misconceived.

Comparative Static Properties

1. An increase in demand will cause an increase in output and in advertising, but price effects will be uncertain. This is Baumol's conclusion, but in fact a fall in output is quite consistent with the equilibrium conditions in the Haveman and DeBartolo version of the model. (If the revenue function in Fig. 4.5 shifts outwards, the intersection with a different cost + advertising + minimum profit curve could yield greater or smaller output and higher or lower price. One cannot even conclude that there will be more advertising.)

2. A lump-sum tax or an increase in fixed cost will lead to a reduction in output and in advertising. This contrasts with a profit maximiser who would maintain both unchanged. In Fig. 4.9 the profit function shifts uniformly downwards and output falls from X_C to X_T. Similarly, the effect on the equilibrium level of advertising can be seen from a downward shift of the profit function of Fig. 4.3. The effect on price cannot be predicted in

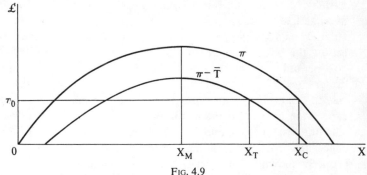

Fig. 4.9

spite of Baumol's emphasis upon this as one of the empirical justifications of his model. With advertising falling as well as output, the sales maximiser will not necessarily raise his price: by itself smaller output implies higher price (given the demand curve), but less advertising shifts demand to the left, leaving the price effect indeterminate.

3. The case of the profits tax is similar. The post-tax profit curve has the same intercepts on the X-axis and reaches a maximum at the same X-value. Again, the sales maximiser reduces output and advertising.

4. A sales tax shifts the profit curve to the left as well as downwards so that both types of firm respond by reducing output. However, the sales maximiser's reduction will be greater, as is shown in Fig. 4.10.

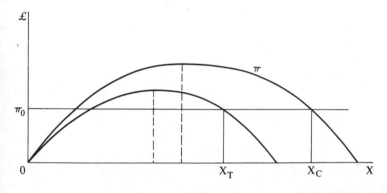

Fig. 4.10

Notice that all these responses rely on the basic assumption that the marginal revenue of advertising is positive, which enables us to assume the constraint π_0 is met precisely. Baumol attached great importance to these conclusions, particularly the second. He thought it an important indication that his model represents the facts of business behaviour more closely than the neoclassical model, since it is true that firms in practice do tend to pass on to the consumer the cost – at least in part – of lump-sum increases. As we have just seen, price does not necessarily rise; nevertheless one could concede Baumol his point merely on the grounds that the sales maximiser may at least consider raising his price (even if he does not always do so) whereas this policy would not even occur to a profit-maximiser who either knew that the derivative of a constant is zero or had digested the dictum that sunk costs cannot be retrieved by an irrational price decision. However, it may be objected that what the Baumol firm does is quite as unrealistic as the textbook profit maximiser (for whom no one in fact claims operational, as opposed to analytical, validity). The rise in price is implicit in Baumol, not explicit. It follows from the reduction in output, which is itself a result of the fall in profit and the need to satisfy the profit constraint again. It is not realistic to suggest that firms reduce output as a matter of policy, only to discover that the particular output associated with the required level of profit is saleable at a higher price. The realistic account of a typical response to a rise in fixed cost would be a mark-up procedure in which price was genuinely determined and output explicitly contingent. But Baumol characterises mark-up rules as indeterminate and inconsistent. It is therefore difficult to claim that his model is more satisfactory as a behavioural exercise than more traditional ones, although it does deliver better predictions about the outcome.

WELFARE

It is claimed[13] that since the sales maximiser's equilibrium output is greater than the profit maximiser's, it follows that it will be closer to the welfare ideal where marginal cost equals price. Even if one ignores the Hawkins point and assumes the sales maximiser does indeed produce more than the profit maximiser, it is not at all clear that the claim can be substantiated. In Fig. 4.11 the situation of the firm in Fig. 4.2 is reproduced in terms of unit cost and revenue. For simplicity of exposition, demand (D), marginal revenue (MR), average variable cost (AVC) and marginal cost (MC) are all linear, leaving average total cost (ATC) exceeding average variable cost by the diminishing amount of average fixed cost (not shown separately). X_W is the ideal output from the point of society as a whole; X_M is monopoly output and X_R that of the unconstrained revenue maximiser where $MR = 0$. X_C the output of the constrained sales maximiser, is determined by the point at which profit ($PQRS$) is reduced to the minimum acceptable level.

The question is whether X_C is better than X_M in the Pareto sense. First, it is clear that, of the two, X_C may be further from X_W in terms of units of output. Second, the welfare loss at X_C from the overallocation of resources to this product may be greater than the loss at X_M from under-allocation. Estimating benefits and costs even in this narrow context of course involves making at least the following heroic assumptions: that the height of the demand curve at any output measures the money value of the satisfaction derived by the consumer; that these satisfactions can be added together to yield a meaningful aggregate; and that the height of the marginal-cost curve measures the cost to society as well as to the firm of the resources used – costs incurred by society on behalf of the firm and benefits conferred by the firm on society being alike ignored. Given all this – which is implicit in Baumol's claim as well as in the counter to it – it is evident that, as is the case in Fig. 4.11, the welfare loss associated with X_C (the area STU) may be greater than that associated with X_M (the area VTZ). Sales maximisers may be even more undesirable than profit-maximising monopolists.

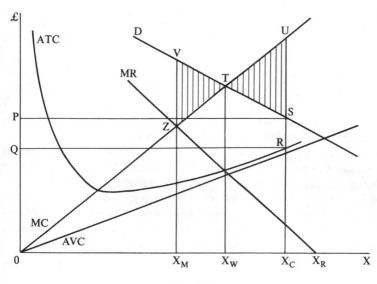

Fig. 4.11

If we look now, not at the equilibrium output level of the sales maximiser but at the relative amounts of various inputs and outputs it uses and produces, we have the proposition:

Given the level of expenditure, the sales-maximising firm will produce the same quantity of each output and market it in the same ways as does the profit maximiser. Similarly, given the level of their total revenues the two types of firm will optimally use the same inputs in identical quantities and will allocate them in exactly the same way.[14]

The reason for this is that the firms will allocate resources in accordance with the same marginal criteria: assuming a given outlay on resources, combinations which yield maximum revenue must also yield maximum profit (revenue minus outlay). Here Baumol is taking another step away from operationality and rule-of-thumb and towards marginalism. The difference between the profit and the sales maximiser will lie not in a different allocation of resources but merely in a different level of output. In other words, given a negative marginal profit, each time the output of some product is increased the firm must use up more of its 'fund of sacrificeable profits'. This must be allocated among the different outputs, markets and inputs in a way which maximises sales. The yield in marginal revenue of a pound of profit sacrificed by all products must be the same: 'Even in the sales-maximising firm relatively unprofitable inputs and outputs are to be avoided.'

However, while it is true that firms fulfil the same marginal criteria, it does not follow that they will use the same resources in the same way: since the sales maximiser's level of advertising and of output will be different from those of the profit maximiser, his optimal input mix will be different (as Fig. 4.6 shows). Furthermore, the tangled web of criteria for maximum welfare cannot be unravelled by the kind of avowedly impressionistic conclusions which Baumol draws – such as that, since there will be widespread divergences from Paretian optimality, then it may be that the distortions cancel out leaving an allocation of resources 'as close to the optimum as can reasonably be expected'. After all, the existence of advertising and imperfectly competitive conditions in general means that the marginalist calculations on resource allocation referred to above are not the 'correct' ones anyway, and it is the purest speculation to suggest any likelihood that the distortions arising from oligopoly sales maximisers' advertising will somehow be less than those from profit maximisers' advertising.

There is one uncomfortable conclusion on welfare. Since lump-sum taxes will tend to be shifted on to the consumer by a sales maximiser, any widespread adoption of such a goal would prevent the prescription of lump-sum taxes as a means of raising revenue without affecting incentives or resource allocation. However, since such taxes are totally unacceptable on grounds of equity, even this crumb of fiscal policy implication will be of doubtful worth.

In spite of its deceptive simplicity the Baumol model represents an imaginative minor revolution in microeconomic theory. Because of lack of evidence supporting or refuting its basic hypothesis, with all its detailed implications, the model must rely for the present upon the intuitively reasonable character of the behaviour it suggests. A general objection is voiced by Alchian:

> If one postulates asset growth or sales maximisation he will explain some cases but reject a lot of others in which that simply does not hold. Similarly attempts to posit asset or sales maximisation subject to a minimum wealth or profit constraint also run into the objection that it implies the firm will not make any sacrifice in sales, no matter how large an increment in wealth would thereby be achievable. Observed behaviour simply does not support that attempted revision of the theory.[15]

This criticism is marred by a confusing use of terms like 'asset growth', 'asset maximisation' and 'wealth'. However, it is certainly true that it is a rather unacceptable implication of the model that (putting it the opposite way to Alchian), provided the profit constraint is not at the time effective, managers would derive extra satisfaction from huge outlays on advertising which brought negligible increases in sales and large reductions in profit.

Baumol's reply would be that there is strong, albeit impressionistic, evidence that sales are an ultimate objective of managers; that when asked how business is, managers invariably reply that sales are increasing; that it is not unusual to find relatively profitable firms some segment of whose sales is highly unprofitable; that any expedient will be tried before surgery; that businessmen have rejected opportunities to increase their profits at the expense of sales; and that in any case one should not expect any model to be relevant to every situation. Greater generality is inherently desirable but very costly:

> A model can only be designed around a specific problem. A model which sheds some light on one situation can be worse than useless in another because elements which can in one case be dismissed as unimportant may in another be crucial.

Peston[16] makes the point that short-run sales maximising at the expense of short-run profit may be simply explained in terms of long-run profit maximisation. This would be the case if it were believed that future demand, and therefore future sales and profit, were an increasing function of current revenue. Thus, to use one of Baumol's examples, a watch distributor continued to supply certain retailers although the revenue he received from them did not cover the cost of selling to them. It would be difficult to decide whether this represented a preference for sales over profits or a belief that persisting with the unprofitable outlets would improve long-run profit.

Peston also considers the likelihood that, in a state of ignorance about its revenue function, the firm will tend to produce more than the profit-maximising output rather than less: the likelihood, in other words, that it will be led in the direction of sales maximisation, not positively preferring sales to profit but in ignorance of the information needed for maximising profit. The factor said to be leading the firm in this direction is change in the cost function over time. If the firm attaches importance to reductions in operating cost, and if technological improvements bring greater cost savings at higher outputs, then the firm will produce a larger output, yielding greater revenue. It should be emphasised, though, that these attempts to gain the maximum benefit from shifts in the cost function are output-oriented, not revenue-oriented: the two goals are complementary for some ranges of output but they are alternatives after a certain point (where $\partial R/\partial X = 0$).

On the question whether sales are an ultimate objective because the economic rewards received by managers are more closely associated with sales than with other measures of corporate performance, several studies have yielded interesting results. Roberts[17] has performed cross-section regression analysis on data from a sample of 77 American firms in 1948–50 to discover that executive incomes are related to size but unrelated to profitability. McGuire,[18] using data for the period 1953–9, came to similar conclusions but in addition found some correlation between executive incomes and sales.

Hall[19] has tested the Baumol hypothesis by investigating the proposition that when profits are above the minimum acceptable level the firm will take steps consciously to increase sales revenue. The study focused on relatively oligopolistic firms taken from the 400 largest United States industrial corporations, data on sales, profits and output being taken from the period 1960–2. The results

> lend no support to the sales revenue maximisation thesis . . . nor do they imply support for the profit-maximisation thesis. If anything they suggest, given the low simple correlation coefficients between sales or its first difference and our formulation of profit constraint, that many other variables such as Williamson's staff expenditures and Cyert and March's organisational slack share in profits above the constraint.

Shepherd[20] argues that sales maximisation cannot explain oligopolistic behaviour. Oligopoly is, by definition, a market form where interdependence between rivals influences decision-making. In these circumstances it has been suggested[21] that the firm behaves as though its demand curve is kinked, assuming that price increases will not be matched by rivals whereas price reductions will be matched. The total revenue and profit functions will also be kinked and marginal revenue will be discontinuous at the relevant output. The more pronounced the kink, the greater the discontinuity and the more likely it is that marginal cost will go through the discontinuity — leading to stability of prices in response to changes in both demand and cost. Shepherd claims that if demand curves are sharply kinked the discontinuity will extend below the output axis, so that total revenue reaches its maximum at the level of output where the kink occurs, as is shown in Fig. 4.12. Output will be X_K whichever objective the firm is pursuing. The more interdependence there is, the less will a

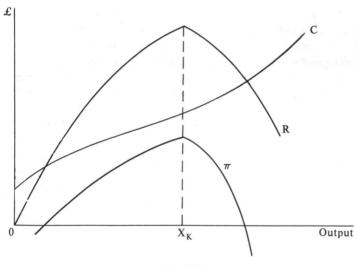

FIG. 4.12

sales objective influence output decisions, since even if the discontinuity in the marginal revenue function does not extend below the output axis, the greater the length of the discontinuity the closer will the profit-maximising output be to the constrained revenue-maximising output.

Shepherd's conclusion is challenged by Hawkins[22] on the ground that it would be valid only in cases where price competition was the only form of competition. Where advertising also occurs, the two types of firm will operate on different demand curves, because they will engage in different amounts of advertising. The necessity of their choosing the same output is removed (even assuming the discontinuity in marginal revenue goes through the output axis). In fact it is possible to go further and show that the Baumol case is reinforced by kinked demand curves. The price charged by both firms is the same – if the kink hypothesis is accepted: this means that higher revenues can be achieved by the sales maximiser as a result of advertising more and producing more. The kink shifts to the right, the increased output being sold at the same price. This precise prediction compares with the imprecise conclusions to be drawn from the Baumol model without kinked demand, where extra advertising could lead to a higher price for a smaller quantity, or even extra output being sold at a lower price with less advertising.

Hawkins points out, however, that the Shepherd analysis causes difficulties in the empirical testing of the Baumol hypothesis. Since both profit maximisers and sales maximisers will equate marginal cost and marginal revenue (but with different cost and revenue functions), a firm could be proved to be sales-maximising only if its level of advertising could be shown to be non-optimal in terms of profit maximisation.

From an entirely different standpoint, doubt has been cast on the Baumol hypothesis by evidence that firms operate at output levels where elasticity of demand is greater than unity and yet where profits greater than the minimum are being earned,[23] which is inconsistent with the equilibrium established in the Baumol model. For if profits greater than the minimum are being earned, the constraint is not effective and elasticity of demand should be unity since the firm will be able to maximise revenue. On the other hand, if the constraint is effective (and this is in fact the assumption) marginal revenue should be positive and elasticity greater than one.

However, the hypothesis is salvaged in ingenious fashion by D. J. Smyth[24] by introducing, in effect, an extra constraint. If managerial effort increases with the scale of operation of the firm, measured by output, and if managers can be assumed to have some aversion to this, we have a managerial utility function in which the benefits accruing to managers from increased sales may be continuously weighed against the cost in terms of effort-requiring output. An indifference curve reflecting managerial effort-aversion would be positively sloped and convex to the X-axis in Fig. 4.2. If a tangency with R occurred to the left of X_C, the 'effort constraint' would be reducing the scale of operations and yielding higher profits. The elasticity of demand would be greater than unity and the profit constraint ineffective. The impact of this suggestion is of course lessened by the small association which exists between scale and the executive work-load. Delegation can ensure that there is little increase in managerial effort: indeed in large firms delegation designed to take the load off higher executives is likely to generate an increase in activity as delegates attempt to justify their income and status.

Managerial effort-aversion is in any case not in line with the dominant theme of most managerial theories (and certainly not with Baumol's theme), which suppose that managerial motivation is entirely concerned with power, prestige and income. On the other hand, the work ethic is fortunately not universal. The positive utilities attached to time spent with the family and to leisure in general may act as a significant brake on an individual's commitment to work. The intriguing possibility emerges that the effort-aversion of managers could produce a level of profit insufficient to satisfy the profit constraint, so that managers would have to work harder in order to survive.[25]

In the nature of things the Baumol hypothesis remains unverified but non-nullified by the evidence. As to that, one would venture the heresy that whether good ideas like Baumol's fit the facts or not (or rather whether they fit a particular subset of the universe of facts or not) is sometimes of small significance compared with the wider possibilities they open up for analysis and investigation. Once one gives up the attempt to formulate a general model in the classical manner, one must expect a model to be as useful for the questions it puts as for any specific answers it might give. The Baumol model certainly asks the right questions. Its main defect is that it falters as an internally consistent system precisely at the point where it attempts to endow the analysis with qualities of realism. Optimising is never 'realistic'.

NOTES AND REFERENCES

1. *Business Behavior, Value and Growth*, p. 27.
2. Ibid., p. 53.

3. The inadequacies of the profit constraint are discussed in D. K. Osborne, 'On the Goals of the Firm', *Quarterly Journal of Economics* (Nov. 1964). The article also expands on a hypothesis (due to F. M. Fisher) that instead of maximising sales subject to a profit constraint, the firm symmetrically maximises profit subject to a sales constraint.

4. H. W. Kuhn and A. Tucker, 'Nonlinear Programming', in J. Neyman (ed.), *Proceedings of the Second Berkeley Symposium on Mathematical Statistics and Probability* (Berkeley: Univ. of California Press, 1951).

5. See T. H. Naylor and J. M. Vernon, *Microeconomics and Decision Models of the Firm* (New York: Harcourt, Brace & World, 1969) p. 151, or I. Horowitz, *Decision Making and the Theory of the Firm* (New York: Holt, Rinehart & Winston, 1970) pp. 258, 297. Only if the global maximum of Z occurred where $X < 0$ would the constrained solution have $\partial Z/\partial X < 0$, as at a in Fig. I. In the present case we are assuming the situation is as shown in Fig. II, with Z maximised at b where $\partial Z/\partial X = 0$ and $X > 0$.

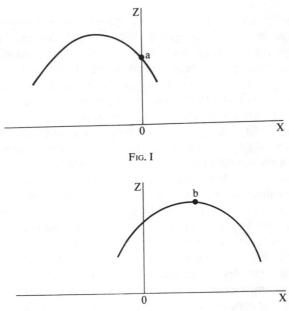

Fig. I

Fig. II

6. In programming terms, λ is the 'shadow price' associated with the constraint. It indicates the rate at which Z would increase as the constraint was relaxed. Clearly, if profit is already greater than necessary, reducing π_0 would not increase R (nor, therefore, Z). Thus $\lambda = 0$. Because of the direction of the inequality in (4.2), when the constraint is effective $\lambda < 0$.

7. R. L. Sandmeyer, 'Baumol's Sales Maximisation Model', *American Economic Review* (Dec. 1964).

8. *Business Behavior*, p. 60.

9. R. Haveman and G. DeBartolo, 'The Revenue Maximising Oligopoly Model: A Comment', *American Economic Review* (Dec. 1968).

10. C. J. Hawkins, 'The Revenue Maximisation Oligopoly Model: Comment', *American Economic Review* (June 1970). The Haveman and DeBartolo analysis is discussed in the same issue of the *A.E.R.* by M. Z. Kafoglis and R. C. Bushnell in a 'Comment' and by Haveman and DeBartolo in a 'Reply'.

11. P. W. S. Andrews, *Manufacturing Business* (London: Macmillan, 1949) p. 184.

12. *Business Behavior*, p. 65.

13. Ibid., p. 76.

14. W. J. Baumol, 'On the Theory of Oligopoly', *Economica* (Aug. 1958).

15. A. A. Alchian, 'The Basis of Some Recent Advances in the Theory of Management of the Firm', *Journal of Industrial Economics* (Nov. 1965).

16. M. H. Peston, 'On the Sales Maximisation Hypothesis', *Economica* (May 1959).

17. D. R. Roberts, *Executive Compensation* (Glencoe, Ill.: Free Press, 1959).

18. J. W. McGuire, J. S. Y. Chiu and A. O. Elbing, 'Executive Incomes, Sales and Profits', *American Economic Review* (Sept. 1962).

19. M. Hall, 'Sales Revenue Maximisation: An Empirical Examination', *Journal of Industrial Economics* (Apr. 1967). This is criticised in L. Waverman, 'Sales Revenue Maximisation: A Note', *Journal of Industrial Economics* (Nov. 1968), where Hall's 'Reply' is also to be found.

20. W. G. Shepherd, 'On Sales Maximising and Oligopoly Behaviour', *Economica* (Nov. 1962).

21. See, for example, G. J. Stigler, 'The Kinky Oligopoly Demand Curve and Rigid Prices', *Journal of Political Economy* (Oct. 1947). Reprinted in G. C. Archibald (ed.) *The Theory of the Firm* (Harmondsworth: Penguin Books 1971).

22. C. J. Hawkins, 'On the Sales Revenue Maximisation Hypothesis', *Journal of Industrial Economics* (Apr. 1970).

23. R. G. Lipsey and P. O. Steiner, *Economics* (New York: Harper & Row, 1966).

24. D. J. Smyth, 'Sales Maximisation and Managerial Effort: Note', *American Economic Review* (Sept. 1969).

25. This possibility may be compared with the suggestion in Chapter 7 (p. 114 below) that firms might in some circumstances have to grow at a faster rate in order to earn a high enough rate of return to survive.

5

MANAGERIAL DISCRETION

O. E. WILLIAMSON'S objectives in *The Economics of Discretionary Behavior* are:

- (*a*) to show in what respects managers' motives lead them to pursue goals other than profit;
- (*b*) to show that the motivation of managers can be related to operational variables which can be incorporated in a formal model;
- (*c*) to develop the equilibrium characteristics and comparative static properties of such a model based on the exercise of managerial discretion; and
- (*d*) to examine the evidence.

Williamson acknowledges his debt to organisation theory, which not only suggested the kinds of phenomenon which might be relevant but also indicated the relationships which would exist between them.

MOTIVES

A substantial consensus exists among organisation theorists, and economists in this field, that the immediate determinants of managerial behaviour are salary, security, status, power, prestige, social service and professional excellence. Of these, status, power and prestige may be grouped together under the notion of dominance. Salary is not a motive in itself but a means to the attainment of security, status, power and prestige. On the other hand, salary is retained as a separate objective because material reward is something the firm is particularly well suited to provide. Social service objectives are ignored for the sake of simplification. The Berlian propositions about corporate conscience are (in my view rightly) rejected because few opportunities normally arise for the pursuit of such goals and because in any case they can probably be explained as attempts to acquire status and prestige for the management, and goodwill (and therefore profit) for the firm.

The following motives then emerge:

1. Salary. —
2. Security.
3. Dominance, embracing:
   (a) status;
   (b) power;
   (c) prestige.
4. Professional excellence.

Of these motives only salary is 'operational', while the rest are non-pecuniary goals. A mechanism is required through which these non-pecuniary goals may be expected to influence the behaviour of the firm. This is provided in the concept of expense preference.

Expense Preference

Some types of expenses have positive values attached to them. They are incurred not merely for their contribution to profitability but also for the manner in which they enhance the individual and collective objectives of managers. The classical assumption that costs are by definition to be minimised at each level of output is therefore abandoned.

(a) *Staff.* It is assumed that management has a positive expense preference for staff, which corresponds to general administrative and selling outlays. Expansion of staff clearly furthers the salary and dominance objectives because it is both a means to, and the equivalent of, promotion. It reduces insecurity because size is a guarantee of survival. It is an index of professional competence.

Thus a tendency to value staff apart from reasons associated with its productivity increases the likelihood that outlay on staff will be pushed beyond the point where its marginal profitability is zero.

(b) *Emoluments.* Emoluments are defined as that portion of management's salaries and perquisites that is discretionary in the sense that they are not part of the entrepreneurial supply price. They are thus economic rents having zero productivity and resulting from the strategic advantage management possesses in the distribution of returns due to monopoly power. Emoluments may be paid either as salary (with the advantage that its use is unrestricted) or as perquisites (which are preferable for tax purposes and because they attract less attention from other groups in the organisation such as shareholders or workers).

Discretionary Profit

This is defined as the amount by which earnings exceed a minimum performance constraint. This is in turn defined as the profit attainment required to prevent shareholders from mobilising their forces for resistance. This profit requirement identical to Baumol's minimum acceptable profit. But whereas in the Baumol model the outlay on staff is assumed always to continue until it has reduced profit to its constrained level, in the Williamson models profits above the minimum have positive utility for two reasons:

1. They make expansion of staff and emoluments possible.
2. Managers derive satisfaction from self-fulfilment and organisational achievement, and profit is a measure of this success.

It is therefore assumed that in the general case the firm is operated so as to maximise a utility function whose principal components are staff, emoluments and discretionary profit, subject to the constraint that reported profit be greater than or equal to the minimum profit demanded.

Staff Model

The first model examines the implications of introducing only staff into the managerial utility function in addition to discretionary profit. In Fig. 5.1 profit is plotted as a function of staff and shown as the curve labelled $\pi = f(S; E)$, which is drawn on the assumption that the condition of the environment is unchanged and that output is chosen optimally. The profit constraint (π_0) could be shown as a horizontal line in the Baumol manner. However, Williamson avoids the problem of maximising subject to a constraint by defining discretionary profit $((1 - t)\pi - \pi_0)$ net of the constraint (t is profit tax) and assuming that it is always positive. If the $\pi = f(S; E)$ curve contracted downwards, its tangency with the S-axis would yield a solution with discretionary profit zero and post-tax profit just equal to π_0.

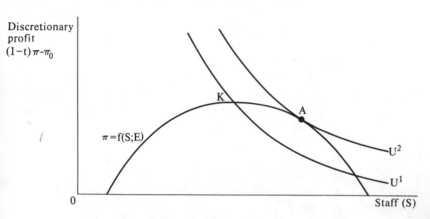

FIG. 5.1

U^1 and U^2 are managerial indifference curves between profit and staff. The point K represents the profit-maximising outcome and A the utility-maximising outcome. If managers have a positive preference for staff, a solution which most pleases shareholders will be less than optimal for managers ($U^1 < U^2$).

A solution at K would require a zero marginal rate of substitution between profit and staff. The indifference curves would be horizontal at that point, indicating that no increase in staff could compensate for a reduction in profit. This could therefore only occur either if the benefits to managers of expanding staff were exhausted before K were reached, or if the marginal utility of staff were always zero except for its contribution to profit. The proximity of A to K, given positive marginal utility of staff, depends on the sharpness of the profit function and the slope of the U curves. Thus the equilibrium of a managerial firm may in various circumstances converge to that of the entrepreneurial firm.

In developing the formal model the following terms are defined:

$U =$ utility function

$X =$ output

$S =$ outlay on staff or general administrative and selling costs (as in Baumol)

$E =$ the condition of the environment, changes in which shift the demand function (demand-shift parameter)

$P =$ price $= P(X, S; E)$. The following relationships are (fairly innocuously) assumed: $\partial P/\partial X < 0$; $\partial P/\partial E > 0$; $\partial P/\partial S \geqslant 0$.

$R =$ revenue or sales $= PX = P(X, S; E) \cdot X$. Thus $R = R(X, S; E)$. It is assumed that $\partial^2 R/\partial X \partial S \geqslant 0$; that is, the effect of increasing staff is to shift the marginal revenue curve to the right or, in the limiting case, to leave it unchanged.

$C =$ production cost $= C(X)$

$\pi =$ actual profit $= R - C - S$

$\pi_0 =$ minimum acceptable post-tax profit

$T =$ taxes which are either profit tax at rate t or lump-sum tax ($\bar{T}$)

$\pi - \pi_0 - T =$ discretionary profit.

The objective then is

maximise $\qquad U = U(S, \pi - \pi_0 - T)$

subject to $\qquad \pi \geqslant \pi_0 + T$.

This could be dealt with, as in the Baumol case (see above, p. 44), by using the Kuhn–Tucker theorem. However, it can be reduced to an unconstrained maximisation problem by assuming that the relative marginal utility of discretionary profit as against staff is never so small as to yield a solution in which discretionary profit is either zero or negative. By normal standards of model-building practice this is a rather strong assumption.[1] However, if the utility function is now written in its complete form

$$U = U[S, (1 - t)(R - C - S - \bar{T}) - \pi_0] \qquad (5.1)$$

it can be seen that U is basically a function of the two independent variables X and S, since R is a function of X and S, and C is a function of X. $\bar{T}$, t and π_0 are parameters.

As a first step to finding the equilibrium characteristics, the total differential of U is given by

$$dU = \frac{\partial U}{\partial S} dS + \frac{\partial U}{\partial [(1-t)(R-C-S-\bar{T})-\pi_0]} d[(1-t)(R-C-S-\bar{T})-\pi_0].$$
(5.2)

Denoting the first partials of U with respect to S and $(1-t)(R-C-S-\bar{T})-\pi_0$ as U_1 and U_2 respectively, we have

$$dU = U_1 . dS + U_2 . d[(1-t)(R-C-S-\bar{T})-\pi_0].$$

From (5.2) the first-order conditions for the maximisation of (5.1) with respect to X and S are given by (5.4) and (5.6) below:

$$\frac{\partial U}{\partial X} = U_1 \frac{\partial S}{\partial X} + U_2 \frac{\partial [(1-t)(R-C-S-\bar{T})-\pi_0]}{\partial X} = 0.$$
(5.3)

Since X and S are independent we have $\partial S/\partial X = 0$, so that

$$U_2(1-t)\left[\frac{\partial R}{\partial X} - \frac{\partial C}{\partial X}\right] = 0$$

which will be satisfied when

$$\frac{\partial R}{\partial X} = \frac{\partial C}{\partial X}$$
(5.4)

And with respect to S, the maximisation of U is given by

$$\frac{\partial U}{\partial S} = U_1 \frac{\partial S}{\partial S} + U_2 \frac{\partial [(1-t)(R-C-S-T)-\pi_0]}{\partial S} = 0$$
(5.5)

that is,

$$U_1 + U_2(1-t)\left(\frac{\partial R}{\partial S} - 1\right) = 0$$

which is satisfied when

$$\frac{\partial R}{\partial S} = 1 - \frac{1}{1-t}\frac{U_1}{U_2} < 1.$$
(5.6)

From (5.4) the firm conventionally equates marginal revenue to marginal cost of production. But from (5.6)

$$\frac{\partial R}{\partial S} < 1$$

that is, the marginal revenue product of staff is less than its marginal

cost, whereas in the profit-maximising model staff would be employed
only to the point where marginal benefit equals marginal cost
($\partial R/\partial S = 1$). The ratio U_1/U_2 is the marginal rate of substitution
between profit and staff which in a profit-maximising firm would be
zero.

Comparative Static Properties of the Staff Model

The comparative static properties are found by investigating how the
system adjusts to a change in the parameters: that is, to a change in
the condition of the environment (E), in the profit-tax rate (t) or in a
lump-sum tax ($\bar{T}$). We need to know the effect of these upon the two
independent variables, X and S.

When a parameter changes it must be treated as a variable, but the
first-order equilibrium conditions (5.3) and (5.5) must continue to hold
since the managers will seek a new utility-maximising position in the
new circumstances. Thus we must still have

$$U_x \left(\equiv \frac{\partial U}{\partial X} \right) = U_x(X, S; E, t, \bar{T}) = 0 \qquad (5.7)$$

$$U_s \left(\equiv \frac{\partial U}{\partial S} \right) = U_s(X, S; E, t, \bar{T}) = 0. \qquad (5.8)$$

We shall illustrate the procedure by investigating the effects on X and
S of an improvement in the environment of the firm. If the value of
parameter E changes, E becomes a variable while t and $\bar{T}$ are held
constant. The total differentials of (5.7) and (5.8) are

$$dU_x = \frac{\partial U_x}{\partial X} dX + \frac{\partial U_x}{\partial S} dS + \frac{\partial U_x}{\partial E} dE$$

$$dU_s = \frac{\partial U_s}{\partial X} dX + \frac{\partial U_s}{\partial S} dS + \frac{\partial U_s}{\partial E} dE.$$

Dividing by the change in E yields

$$\frac{\partial U_x}{\partial E} = \frac{\partial U_x}{\partial X} \frac{\partial X}{\partial E} + \frac{\partial U_x}{\partial S} \frac{\partial S}{\partial E} + \frac{\partial U_x}{\partial E} = 0 \qquad (5.9)$$

$$\frac{\partial U_s}{\partial E} = \frac{\partial U_s}{\partial X} \frac{\partial X}{\partial E} + \frac{\partial U_s}{\partial S} \frac{\partial S}{\partial E} + \frac{\partial U_s}{\partial E} = 0 \qquad (5.10)$$

and therefore, since, for example,

$$\frac{\partial U_x}{\partial X} = \frac{\partial(\partial U/\partial X)}{\partial X} = \frac{\partial^2 U}{\partial X^2}$$

then

$$\frac{\partial^2 U}{\partial X^2}\frac{\partial X}{\partial E} + \frac{\partial^2 U}{\partial X \partial S}\frac{\partial S}{\partial E} = -\frac{\partial^2 U}{\partial X \partial E}$$

$$\frac{\partial^2 U}{\partial S \partial X}\frac{\partial X}{\partial E} + \frac{\partial^2 U}{\partial S^2}\frac{\partial S}{\partial E} = -\frac{\partial^2 U}{\partial S \partial E}. \tag{5.11}$$

We thus have a system of two equations in two variables, $\partial X/\partial E$ and $\partial S/\partial E$. The solution for $\partial X/\partial E$ and $\partial S/\partial E$ is given by

$$\begin{bmatrix} \left(\dfrac{\partial X}{\partial E}\right)^0 \\[2ex] \left(\dfrac{\partial S}{\partial E}\right)^0 \end{bmatrix} = \frac{1}{D}\begin{bmatrix} \dfrac{\partial^2 U}{\partial S^2} & -\dfrac{\partial^2 U}{\partial X \partial S} \\[2ex] -\dfrac{\partial^2 U}{\partial X \partial S} & \dfrac{\partial^2 U}{\partial X^2} \end{bmatrix}\begin{bmatrix} -\dfrac{\partial^2 U}{\partial X \partial E} \\[2ex] -\dfrac{\partial^2 U}{\partial S \partial E} \end{bmatrix} \tag{5.12}$$

where $(\partial X/\partial E)^0$ and $(\partial S/\partial E)^0$ denote derivatives at X^0 and S^0, the equilibrium values of X and S, and where

$$D \equiv \begin{vmatrix} \dfrac{\partial^2 U}{\partial X^2} & \dfrac{\partial^2 U}{\partial X \partial S} \\[2ex] \dfrac{\partial^2 U}{\partial X \partial S} & \dfrac{\partial^2 U}{\partial S^2} \end{vmatrix}.$$

The values of $\partial X/\partial E$ and $\partial S/\partial E$ can be obtained, without particularising the functional relationships, from the signs of the expressions in equation (5.12). Taking in turn the three parts of the right-hand side of (5.12):

(*a*) The second-order condition for maximum U is $D > 0$.
(*b*) The sign matrix D is

$$D = \begin{vmatrix} - & + \\ + & - \end{vmatrix}$$

if one assumes firstly that there is diminishing marginal utility of both X and S (the indifference curves in Fig. 5.1 are convex to the origin) and secondly that $\partial R/\partial S$ increases with X causing $\partial U/\partial S$ to increase with X; that is, the marginal revenue productivity of staff is greater at higher levels of output than at lower levels. The four elements of the inverse matrix are therefore negative.

(c) The signs of the second partials of U with respect to variable and parameter are

$$\frac{\partial^2 U}{\partial X \partial E} > 0 \qquad \text{and} \qquad \frac{\partial^2 U}{\partial S \partial E} > 0$$

for which the justification is also intuitive. As the environment becomes more munificent, an increment of output or of staff yields a greater increase in revenue than it would under less favourable conditions.

Substitution of these results into (5.12) gives the comparative static responses

$$\left(\frac{\partial X}{\partial E}\right)^0 > 0, \qquad \left(\frac{\partial S}{\partial E}\right)^0 > 0.$$

Repetition of this procedure for the parameters t and $\bar{T}$ requires that similar assumptions be made about the signs of the second partials, and Williamson asserts that the following are reasonable:

$$\frac{\partial^2 U}{\partial X \partial t} = 0, \qquad \frac{\partial^2 U}{\partial X \partial \bar{T}} = 0$$

and

$$\frac{\partial^2 U}{\partial S \partial t} > 0(?), \qquad \frac{\partial^2 U}{\partial S \partial \bar{T}} < 0.$$

If this is accepted, the complete response for the staff model is

		Parameter		
		E	t	T
Variable	X^0	$+$	$+(?)$	$-$
	S^0	$+$	$+(?)$	$-$

Thus taxes of either kind evoke a response different from that of the profit maximiser and different from each other: a profits tax probably increases preference for staff and this implies that the optimal output increases also. The output response is in the same direction as the staff response because it is entirely derived from it. A lump-sum tax causes both output and staff outlay to fall.

Income and Substitution Effects in the Staff Model

The ambiguity of response to an increase in t can be explained in terms of the income and substitution effects on one component of the utility function, S, of a rise in the 'price' or market transformation rate of the other, $(1 - t)\pi - \pi_0$. By definition the substitution effect is positive if the components are substitutes; the income effect is negative (S falls as t rises) unless outlay on staff is an inferior good. The overall effect depends on which of the two effects is larger. In Fig. 5.2 the profit function in the absence of profit tax is shown as $t = 0$. Equilibrium is at A on U^2. If the tax rate is $t_1 > 0$ the profit function becomes $t = t_1$, which has a smaller slope than $t = 0$ at every level of S. The new equilibrium is at C on U^1. In principle C may lie either to the right or to the left of A — hence the ambiguity.

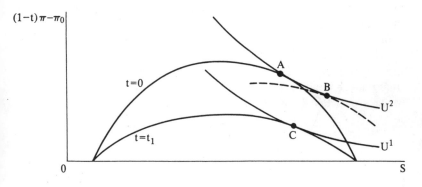

Fig. 5.2

In terms of conventional indifference analysis, profit has become relatively more costly. We may assume the substitution effect to be positive since the two components of the utility function are substitutes. AB is the substitution effect, separated out from the income effect by means of a compensating variation in profit (in the Hicks sense) which, starting from C, produces the dotted line which is a vertical displacement of $t = t_1$. AB is positive because $t = t_1$ is flatter than $t = 0$.

BC is the income effect. If BC were positive or zero the rise in t would undoubtedly cause an increase in S. But for C to occur at the same S-value as B would require U^1 to be a vertical displacement of U^2 (since $t = t_1$ is a vertical displacement of the dotted line); while if C

occurred at a greater S-value, U^1 would have to be steeper than U^2: the lower the level of profit the greater the marginal utility of staff. However, it is much more likely that the lower the level of profit the greater the increase in staff required to compensate for a given reduction in profit, while still maintaining the same level of utility. If this is accepted, it means that U^1 is less steep than U^2, C lies to the left of B and the ambiguity about the direction of AC remains. If C were to the right of B, staff would be an inferior good.— a decrease in funds causing more of it to be bought. Williamson argues that the assumption that staff is not an inferior good, and with it the ambiguity, should remain. However, the income effect is almost always much smaller than the substitution effect. The increase in t will normally increase S (as in Fig. 5.2), but if profits are so low that the constraint is difficult to satisfy, the flattening of the indifference curves will be marked and S could fall. This conclusion would seem to be reasonable since, by definition, expense preference is a feature of situations where 'competitive conditions are not typically severe'.

The effect of a lump-sum tax T is to shift the profit curve vertically downwards in Fig. 5.2. If similar assumptions are granted about the marginal rate of substitution of staff for profit, then the tangency at C occurs at a lower value for staff.

THE EMOLUMENTS MODEL

An emoluments term (M) is substituted for the staff term. The function to be maximised becomes

$$U = U[M, (1 - t)(R - C - S - M - \overline{T}) - \pi_0]$$

and U is a function of three independent variables X, S and M. First-order conditions are

$$\frac{\partial R}{\partial X} = \frac{\partial C}{\partial X} \tag{5.13}$$

$$\frac{\partial R}{\partial S} = 1 \tag{5.14}$$

$$U_1 = (1 - t)U_2 \tag{5.15}$$

where

$$U_1 = \frac{\partial U}{\partial M}$$

and

$$U_2 = \frac{\partial U}{\partial [(1-t)(R-C-S-M-\bar{T})-\pi_0]}.$$

From (5.13) and (5.14) the behaviour of the firm is conventional and it will maximise profit (as at K in Fig. 5.1). But, from (5.15), the firm will absorb some part of actual profit as rent, and reported profit on which tax is levied will be less than the maximum.

The comparative static responses, derived in the same manner as the staff model, are

	E	t	$\bar{T}$
X^0	$+$	0	0
S^0	$+$	0	0
M^0	$+$	$+(?)$	$-$

The explanation of the ambiguous response of the emoluments term to a profits tax is similar to that given above for the staff model. The effect can normally be expected to be positive unless the firm approaches close to its minimum profit constraint.

THE STAFF AND EMOLUMENTS MODEL

The function to be maximised is

$$U = U[S, M, (1-t)(R-C-S-M-\bar{T})-\pi_0].$$

The first-order conditions are

$$\frac{\partial R}{\partial X} = \frac{\partial C}{\partial X}$$

$$\frac{\partial R}{\partial S} = \frac{-U_1 + (1-t)U_3}{(1-t)U_3} \tag{5.16}$$

so that

$$\frac{\partial R}{\partial S} = 1 - \frac{1}{(1-t)}\frac{U_1}{U_3} < 1 \tag{5.17}$$

and

$$U_2 = (1-t)U_3 \tag{5.18}$$

where U_1 is the first partial of U with respect to S, U_2 is the first partial with respect to M and U_3 the first partial with respect to $(1 - t)(R - C - S - M - \bar{T}) - \pi_0$. These equations reveal that the equilibrium characteristics of the previous models are maintained. Although the amount of profit absorbed as emoluments affects the level of discretionary profit, it has no direct effect on productivity.

The comparative static responses are

	E	t	$\bar{T}$
X^0	+	+(?)	−
S^0	+	+(?)	−
M^0	+	+(?)	−

SUMMARY OF RESULTS FOR WILLIAMSON MODELS

The conclusions are presented for the staff and emoluments model:

1. As is the case for a profit maximiser, staff outlays, emoluments and output all vary directly with the condition of the environment. In the limit, as the environment deteriorates, the firm's use of staff converges to its profit-maximising value, and profit-absorbing emoluments are reduced. This conforms to the Baumol predictions.

2. Spending on both staff and emoluments increases with an increase in the profits-tax rate. Output also increases because the increase in S leads to an increase in the optimal value of X. This contrasts with the profit maximiser's complete lack of response. It also contrasts with the prediction of the Baumol model that an increase in profits tax will cause a reduction in staff and output. This is because the minimum profit constraint in Baumol is assumed to be always binding, so that any increase in taxes requires the firm to forgo revenues and move its decision variables towards a profit-maximising position.

3. Contrary to traditional theory, changes in fixed cost do influence the firm. A lump-sum tax reduces reported profit; a reduction in emoluments will counter this by increasing reported profit, while a reduction in staff has the same effect through an increase in actual profit. That is, since in this case there is no substitution

effect, the response consists entirely of the negative income effect on the assumption that the marginal rate of substitution diminishes. This result also agrees with Baumol's.

An interesting difference arises between the welfare implications of the Baumol and the Williamson models. In the Baumol case, as we have seen, it is argued that the expansion of output of the sales maximiser may mean smaller welfare losses due to under-allocation of resources to oligopolists. In the managerial discretion model, expansion occurs only as a result of the positive preference for staff and the output response is indirect. If increasing staff and advertising outlays, by developing more clear-cut differentiation of products, should make the demand curve more inelastic as it shifts to the right, then the model may be characterised by increases in price rather than increases in output. The welfare effects would be much less desirable.

In general, of course, the discretion models suffer from the inability to offer pricing implications which afflicts all models except perfect competition: once price becomes a decision variable, no model which specifies general rather than precise functional relationships can predict price decisions.

As for empirical evidence that managerial discretion influences behaviour, Williamson used two methods. In the first, field studies of firms experiencing adverse business conditions showed the extent to which adjustments in staff and emoluments would support the predictions of the model. The use of the 'extreme instance' is a way of avoiding *ceteris paribus* qualifications which could only be ruled out in principle by conducting a controlled experiment: 'In short, although the *cetera* are never *paria*, it may be possible to treat them as if they were by restricting the analysis to observations of the extreme instance variety.'[2] Overwhelming evidence was found of cost-reducing activities in times of declining profit.

The second method used was statistical analysis of cross-section data for the two largest firms in each of 26 industries for the years 1953, 1957 and 1961. The evidence suggested that

> managerial objectives have a systematic influence on the operations of the firm and that conditions of competition in the product market play a critical role in determining the extent to which discretionary behaviour is quantitatively important.[3]

The acceptance of a non-profit goal is now so widespread in the theory of the firm that complaints about 'economists' reluctance to take the concept seriously'[4] seem rather like over-protestation. Rather is it appropriate to emphasise that the profit goal is still relevant. Maximum profit remains at worst a standard point of reference, an identifiable outcome against which other outcomes may be set for comparison.

More than this, the status of the classical or entrepreneurial model should not be considered impaired by the emergence of managerial models. It is a perfectly suitable model for competitive conditions: indeed the other models tend to converge upon it as the survival of the firm is threatened. It is also the basis for analysis of monopolistic situations where because of regulatory constraint neither the maximising of profit nor the exercise of managerial discretion is acceptable – for example, public utility operation. When the focus of interest is elsewhere than on the owner–manager relationship, the profit-maximising assumption is the best because it is the simplest. For example, when the problem is the efficient use of resources so that the cost of a given output is minimised; or the setting-up of valid investment criteria; or the evaluation of alternative strategies when the outcomes are uncertain because of rivals' reactions; then to adopt a complex managerial utility function would divert attention from essentials. Thus since it is the most economical model in terms of assumptions made and apparatus required, it is often the most efficient tool to use.

In this connection Williamson has himself provided an interesting sequel to his managerial theory[5] in which, if he does not stand that theory completely on its head, he takes a dramatically different view of contemporary capitalism. He claims that large corporations now conform quite closely to the neoclassical profit-maximisation hypothesis. The pursuit of managerial goals arises out of the control-loss phenomenon in large multifunctional companies with a unitary organisation (the U-firm). The organisation of the firm into functional divisions increases the likelihood that heads of divisions will pursue non-profit-maximising goals, since the divisions will have conflicting sub-goals. But there is a response to these problems of co-ordination. This is the multidivisional firm (the M-firm) with quasi-autonomous operating divisions organised mainly on product or geographical lines. The M-firm favours goal pursuit and least-cost behaviour more nearly associated with profit maximisation than does the U-firm. It promotes competition in product markets, provides an internal substitute for the capital market, and in general contributes to the efficient working of the system. If Williamson's later thesis is accepted, the need for 'managerial' explanations of the behaviour of large firms is becoming less, as also is the need for anti-monopoly intervention by governments.

NOTES AND REFERENCES

1. In terms of Fig. 5.1 it means ruling out a set of indifference curves which 'flatten out' outside the positive quadrant, as in Fig. III. The preference for staff is in this case

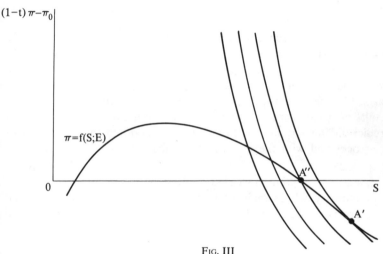

$(1-t)\,\pi-\pi_0$

$\pi=f(S;E)$

A''

A'

0   S

FIG. III

so high and the marginal utility of discretionary profit correspondingly low that U is maximised at A' where $(1 - t)\pi - \pi_0 < 0$. The constrained solution is at A''. Williamson's argument is:

> 'Assuming diminishing marginal utility and disallowing corner solutions, it follows that the firm will always choose values of its decision variables that will yield positive utility with respect to each component of its utility function.' (p. 40.)

The solution at A' satisfies these requirements and is not unreasonable or unlikely. Management still has a positive preference for discretionary profit, but this is overridden by a stronger preference for staff. Neither A' nor A'' therefore deserves to be assumed away, except for the explicit reason that their exclusion makes the analysis significantly easier.

2. O. E. Williamson, *The Economics of Discretionary Behavior*, p. 87.
3. Ibid., p. 167.
4. Ibid.
5. O. E. Williamson, *Corporate Control and Business Behavior*.

6

INTRODUCTION TO
GROWTH THEORY

BOTH from a macroeconomic and a microeconomic standpoint one ought to have a theory of the growth of firms. Presumably the growth of the economic system as a whole does not proceed in some mysterious fashion independently of the growth of its constituent parts. Nor can macroeconomic policies on growth operate with the results of static microeconomic theory when a dynamic theory would predict different behaviour. For there is little doubt that management is preoccupied with the growth of the firm:

> A stationary optimum would doubtless be abhorrent to the captains of industry whose main concern is surely not at what size their enterprise should finally settle down but rather how rapidly to grow.[1]

Once a secure minimum level of earnings has been reached, the technostructure chooses as its goal 'the greatest possible rate of corporate growth as measured in sales'.[2] A theory of the growth of firms could help to explain the divergence between the competitive ideal and capitalism as it actually is. It can also help solve problems which traditional theory has either not raised at all (such as diversification and profit retention) or has treated in an unsatisfactory way (such as advertising). It may incidentally modify the conclusions of the static theory of resource allocation. On the other hand, it should be stressed that growth theories need not necessarily be managerial theories: even if the criterion is to maximise shareholder utility, an optimum growth rate needs to be determined.

But one problem is the extent to which a traditional profit goal and a growth goal would diverge. In the static case there is no conceptual difficulty in the relationship between scale of operations, sales and profitability. Up to a certain scale, profits and sales both increase with size. Beyond that point sales increase with scale but profits decline. When a further well-defined output is reached, sales also begin to decrease. In a multi-period or growth model the relationship is less apparent.

Galbraith, for example, resisting the suggestion that growth may be the best long-run strategy for maximising profits, asserts that the two goals require different policies: he needs this assertion about the effects of growth policies to reinforce his notion of the 'paradox of modern economic motivation'. This is that traditional theory requires the manager to subordinate his interest to that of a remote shareholder, whereas growth as a goal 'is wholly consistent with the personal and pecuniary interest of those who participate in decisions'.[3] Meade produces the familiar argument that high profits are essential for the finance of growth whether by the issue of shares or by undistributed profit: 'The company which desires to expand must therefore seek out profitable fields for its expansion.'[4] However, he does concede that profit policies need not exactly resemble growth policies, and indeed refers to the take-over threat to firms which sacrifice profit to unprofitable growth. The implication is that, take-over apart, after a certain point faster growth reduces profit.

Mrs Penrose, on the other hand, expresses fairly precisely contradictory views. She considers that maximisation of growth is equivalent to maximisation of the absolute size of annual gross profits: 'Firms will never invest in expansion for the sake of growth if the return on investment is negative for that would be self-defeating.'[5] The trouble is that in a growth context the notion of profit (and hence of the maximisation of profit) becomes elusive unless carefully defined. It is better to concentrate on the stock-market value of the firm. Static theories have tended to ignore this crucial link between the corporation and its owners. To maximise profit can only mean to maximise the present value of a stream of profits which in some sense accrues to shareholders whether it is paid out in dividends or used to increase the firm's stock of productive assets. The market price of a share will be the present value of a portion of the stream, and the market value of the firm will be the present value of the whole stream. So profit maximisation means maximisation of the market value of the firm, which is presumed to be what shareholders wish.

STEADY STATE GROWTH

Further clarification of the situation requires the introduction of the concept of steady-state growth, which is implicit but not explicit in the conflicting statements about profitability and growth. Steady-state growth means that the firm is assumed to be choosing once and for all the constant rate at which it will grow indefinitely. The environment in which it operates is in some sense constant and the firm has to adopt a long-run policy, which is a choice of a set of values for those variables through which it responds to its static environment or tries to change it. Such a policy will produce for the firm a steady state in which the variables either grow at a common constant rate (for example assets) or, since they are ratios between other variables, remain constant (for example the valuation ratio, which is the ratio of market value of the firm to assets).

There are several justifications for the steady-state approach. It is convenient analytically because it avoids use of the calculus of variations which is required for a treatment of non-steady paths. It is also more reasonable the longer the time period: optimal non-steady paths tend to converge to steady paths so that firms following optimal paths will tend to grow steadily in the long run.[6] It is true that the empirical evidence does not suggest stability of growth rates but on the contrary indicates considerable variation in the growth rates of individual firms from one five-year period to the next. The way round this objection is to

> regard these theories as determining the expected (in the sense of most likely) long-run growth rate of the firm, knowing that the expectation is surrounded by a high degree of uncertainty. The policy of the firm can thus be said to determine a probability distribution of growth rates which in practice has a rather high variance.[7]

Fig. 6.1, taken from *The Corporate Economy*, illustrates the steady-state path of a joint-stock corporation growing at 5 per cent per annum, with an average reported profit rate of 10 per cent, a retention ratio of 50 per cent and a valuation ratio of 2·0.

Different paths, all permanent, all sustainable, will have different policies: for example, a lower growth rate might be associated with a higher rate of return and a lower retention ratio, leading to a higher valuation ratio. What has to be investigated is the relationship between these different paths. Thus, given a growth rate, g, total profit will, along with the other variables, grow at the rate g. In that context it will therefore make sense to say that growth always increases aggregate profit. The question is whether a different growth rate would have allowed aggregate profit to increase faster.

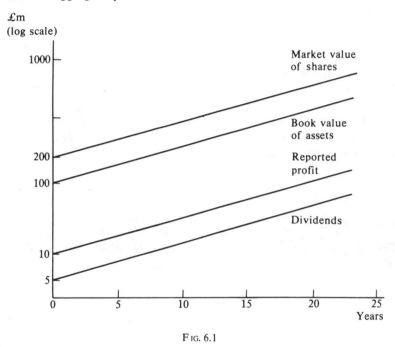

FIG. 6.1

A distinction has to be made between investment decisions and output decisions. Given the stock of capital and the managerial team, there is no difficulty about asserting that to maximise current profit will maximise the funds available for future growth. Investment decisions cause more trouble. If the firm's cost of capital is interpreted as the rate of discount which should be applied to the stream of earnings expected to flow from an investment project, then to undertake investments whose rate of return is less than the cost of capital must reduce the flow of net earnings (profit) in favour of an increase in the current scale of operations. To have maximised profit would have maximised the availability of funds but would have restricted the projects that could be undertaken. Thus, given an environment where the opportunities for profitable investment are exhausted, with consequent increase in the costs of diversification, the marginal rate of return may have to fall below the cost of capital if growth is to occur at a faster rate. Managers will thus in general have some discretion to finance a higher rate of growth from retentions than the shareholders would prefer because it is at the expense of profit.

On the other hand, investment opportunities may be so promising that internal funds can be exhausted without pushing the rate of return below shareholders' opportunity cost.[8] No conflict of interest on retention policy then arises between managers and shareholders – a state of affairs characteristic of firms in the early stages of their life-cycle. Of course, once this stage is over, the conflict appears: managerial pursuit of growth will then be constrained by stock-market disapproval expressed in the form of a fall in the market value of the firm and an increasing danger of being taken over.

COSTS

Following the pattern set by Baumol and J. H. Williamson, we shall divide costs into two categories:

(a) Ordinary production and operating costs: that is, any costs which would be associated with a given level of output if the rate of output were not changing. These would include, for example, marketing outlays designed to maintain the demand for the firm's products intact in the face of competitive pressures.

(b) Expansion costs or development costs: any additional outlays, above and beyond operating costs, which arise only as a result of the expansion process. Examples of such outlays would be investment in capital assets, outlay on additional managers and their integration into the managerial team, and marketing expenditures designed to shift the demand curve for the firm's products.

The operating profit is therefore the profit which would be earned if the firm incurred no expenditure on growth. The reported profit of a growing firm is operating profit less expansion costs. These definitions would allow for a firm to grow without incurring expansion costs if there were autonomous growth in the economy from which it benefited. In the long run the size of the firm will be unconstrained: assuming constant returns to scale – as generated for example by a linear homogeneous production function with constant input prices – operating costs increase proportionately with output. For a single-product firm, if profits and sales are to grow at the same rate as output the higher output must be sold at the same price – implying perfectly elastic demand for the firm's product. In such a static model there would be no equilibrium output, as is seen from Fig. 6.2.

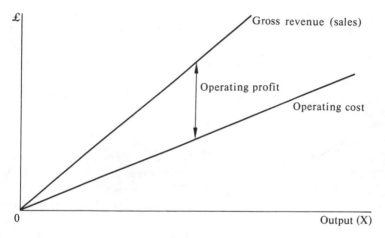

F ɪɢ. 6.2

When we consider oligopoly, steady-state growth as defined above implies a multi-product firm since the expanding output of a single, differentiated product would not be sold at a constant price, even with growing advertising outlay. (Although Marris claims that even a single-product firm could rely on the cumulative effects of advertising in the long run, so that a constant marketing expenditure per unit of sales could sustain a constant growth rate of sales with constant selling prices.) With a multi-product firm – that is, with growth through diversification occurring – the concepts of physical volume of output and constant price are less applicable and the requirement for balanced growth is a steady increase in sales revenue or, even more generally, a steady increase in total profit. This should be attainable:

'A firm expanding by diversification should be able to diversify continuously, at a steady rate over time, without necessarily adversely affecting profitability.'[9]

We are thus saying that, in principle, for at least some large oligopolists (and probably for most) there are no static constraints upon the size of the firm. Unit operating costs tend to be constant and, as far as the market for the expanding output is concerned, diminishing marginal effectiveness of advertising cannot be relied on to produce an optimum size.

DYNAMIC CONSTRAINTS

The annual rate at which the firm can grow towards its infinitely large potential size is, however, constrained. In principle the constraints may be classified as either 'supply' constraints or 'demand' constraints.

Supply

The efficiency of the firm is reduced if the rate of growth is too high. This is the so-called Penrose effect. It is impossible for a firm to expand efficiently beyond a certain point merely by drawing up a plan for a larger organisation and then hiring people to fill the various positions. If a firm deliberately or inadvertently expands its organisation more rapidly than the individuals in the expanding organisation can obtain the experience with each other that is necessary for the effective operation of the group, the efficiency of the firm will suffer in the sense that the capital–output ratio will rise. The capacities of the existing managerial personnel of the firm thus set a limit to the expansion rate of the firm over any given period of time.

Thus we can assume that as the scale of the firm (K) increases steadily at rate g, total expansion costs (G) increase, also at g. If these costs are 'normalised' – that is, expressed as costs per unit of scale – then G/K is constant. The Penrose effect implies that, for example, to double the rate of growth of assets and of the managerial team would not achieve a doubling of output because of a rise in operating costs due to lower efficiency. Thus as G/K increases, g – in the sense of sustainable growth in output – increases less than proportionately. To put it the other way round, G/K is an increasing function of g and furthermore increases more than proportionately. The Penrose effect therefore implies

$$G/K = f(g), \quad \frac{d(G/K)}{dg} > 0$$

$$\frac{d^2(G/K)}{dg^2} > 0.$$

In view of the other restraints on growth, $d^2(G/K)/dg^2 > 0$ is neither a sufficient nor a necessary condition for the achievement of an equilibrium rate of growth. Diminishing returns in this organisational sense would not lead to a constraint on growth, for instance, if there were more significant increasing returns on the 'demand' side. Constant returns in the organisational sense would not prevent demand or finance problems from generating a constraint. The most likely situation, though, is that all three restraining influences will operate.[10]

But even if the efficiency factor did not operate, a further 'supply' constraint arises from the fact that the growth of the capital stock must be financed and that the supply of finance is limited. Whether the firm grows by internal or external finance, the rate of profit it is earning, together with the rate of growth it is trying to achieve, affect the price of shares and the financial security of the organisation. This is dealt with later in this chapter and in Chapter 7.

Demand

Balanced growth, as we have seen, requires sales to increase continuously without falling profitability. We have to imagine, instead of the traditional demand curve for the single product of the firm, a demand curve or function for the corporation. Because of the already-mentioned difficulties of aggregating the prices and quantities of different products, the dimensions of this demand curve would be, not price and quantity, but total profit and total capacity. Assuming that the firm, in addition to its other decisions, has made the optimal static choice of the outputs of a fixed catalogue of products, the demand curve would define a frontier of maximum profits for every indicated level of assets. Static profit maximising would imply choosing the highest point on this curve, assuming one existed.

Growth implies shifting the demand curve and increasing the number of products in the catalogue by expenditures on research, development and marketing. As with expansion costs on the 'supply' side, total development costs will increase with size. A constant proportionate expenditure on demand creation (again, as before, normalised by assets) will be assumed to produce a constant growth rate in demand. Normalised growth-creating expenditure will be an increasing function of the growth rate and will be subject to diminishing effectiveness – that is, we assume 'dynamic diminishing returns'.

The detailed implications of these assumptions will be worked out in the next chapter. The sequence, however, is fairly clear at this stage. At too high a rate of growth the difficulties associated with diversification into new markets, combined with the lower efficiency of management, lead to a fall in the profit rate. The growth of assets, output and sales is being financed either by increasing retentions or by new issues of stock or by borrowing. But higher fund-raising combined with a lower rate of profit lead to stock-market disapproval which limits growth. In such a climate there is in principle a lower growth rate (g^*), acceptable to shareholders, which could be sustained indefinitely, given no change in the environment. Given g^*, the output and scale of the firm in any particular period is determined, provided the initial output is known.[11]

FINANCIAL POLICY

The most important fund-raising decisions are usually thought to be (a) the allocation of profit between dividends and retained earnings and (b) the quantity of outside capital which should be raised either by issuing shares (equity capital) or borrowing (debt finance or bonds). However, we shall actually find that, provided we make certain explicit and challengeable assumptions, it makes no difference how funds are raised. Even without these assumptions it will be possible, and highly convenient, to nominate a single financial policy variable (the retention ratio) whose value is to be determined in accordance with the objectives being pursued.

In principle, then, the choice of a financial policy involves at least:

1. Determining the optimum ratio of debt to assets (leverage or gearing).
2. Determining the optimum balance between internal and external funds.

The implication is that the optimal financial policy maximises the total funds available: with retentions at a high level, an increase in dividends is so welcomed by the market that the loss of internal funds is more than made up by the cheapening of external funds. But as payout ratios become higher this is subject to diminishing returns. Total funds are thus limited and depend on the financial policy chosen.

Debt

Because bonds have a prior claim on company earnings they are usually considered to entail less risk to the investor than shares, and therefore the interest cost to the firm of raising funds in this way is less. Thus for a given investment project, the greater the proportion of funds raised by issuing bonds the greater the share of the returns enjoyed by current shareholders (provided the rate of return on the investment is greater than the rate of interest on the debt). However, the risk which the bondholder is not undertaking is being borne by the shareholder, who feels the full effects of any fall in company earnings.

In ignoring, as we do, the problem of this gearing ratio, we may rely on either of two mutually exclusive procedures: we can either assume away the market imperfections which alone give rise to the problem; or we can admit the imperfections and assume that an optimal solution has been found. We shall use the latter. Thus whatever decisions are made about finance from other sources, we assume an optimal, constant gearing: faster, sustainable growth will not be achieved by borrowing more.[12]

Share Issues and the Value of the Firm

This section relies to a considerable extent on Marris's 'An Introduction to Theories of Corporate Growth' in *The Corporate Economy*. Similar results were earlier derived by J. H. Williamson in his 1966 article, but the Marris version is more economical.

In a steady-state growth model with no uncertainty, dividend growth is the only source of growth in the capital value of an investor's holding in the firm. Sale of a share at a certain point in time leaves the investor with the dividends already received plus a lump sum which is the capitalised value of the expected future dividends. Unless dividends and capital gains are taxed differently, the investor will be indifferent between them and we may base the valuation of the firm solely on the expected dividends.

We thus wish to find an expression for the current value of an annual dividend d, which is expected with certainty to grow at a rate of g_d per cent per annum indefinitely. The amount an investor would be prepared to pay for such a stream of payments will reflect the fact that on the one hand the sums paid out will increase year by year, but on the other hand future payments are not as desirable as present ones and the more distant in time the less desirable they are. This is mainly because of uncertainty about the future. For the moment we assume no uncertainty so that investors simply 'discount' the future at a constant rate of i per cent. This means that in a certain world where a sum received and invested now will earn an interest at i per cent, the same sum delayed for a year will be worth less now. An amount d_0 invested now will have increased to $d_0(1 + i) = d_1$ after one year. If $d_1 = d_0(1 + i)$, it follows that $d_0 = d_1/(1 + i)$, where in the present context d_1 is a payment expected next year and d_0, the present value, is to be found. If d_2 is a payment to be made in two years' time its present value is $d_2/(1 + i)^2$, and if it is to be made in t years it is worth now $d_t/(1 + i)^t$. Thus with a constant dividend d there would be a stream of values

$$\frac{d}{1 + i} + \frac{d}{(1 + i)^2} + \cdots + \frac{d}{(1 + i)^t} \cdot$$

This is a geometric progression with first term $d/(1 + i)$ and common ratio $1/(1 + i)$. With first term a and common ratio r, the sum of t terms is

$$S_t = a\frac{1 - r^t}{1 - r} \cdot$$

The series converges to $a/(1 - r)$ as t approaches infinity, provided that r is numerically less than unity so that $1 - r^t$ approaches 1. In our case the present value converges to

$$\frac{\dfrac{d}{1 + i}}{1 - \dfrac{1}{1 + i}} = \frac{d}{i} \cdot$$

However, the dividend is not in fact constant but is growing at a constant rate g_d. We can treat the growth rate as negative interest[13] so that the present value of the dividend stream is

$$\frac{d}{i - g_d} \cdot$$

On the assumptions made, then, the market value of the stream of dividends will, like that of a perpetual bond, be found by dividing the annual amount receivable by the current market rate of discount — except that in this case the discount rate is 'net' in that it allows for steady growth in the annual payments. But notice that if $g_d > i$ there is no convergence and the present value will be infinite. This possibility (the 'growth stock paradox') is usually assumed away on the ground that if the value of some shares showed any tendency to become infinite, the discount rate, reflecting the opportunity cost of capital, would necessarily rise so as to restore equilibrium. If the discount rate is truly exogenous for the individual firm,[14] we are forced to rely on simple assertion that the growth rate will not be allowed to exceed the discount rate in our models.

If we define $1/(i - g_d)$ as the 'present value function' for the particular case we are considering, it is clear that, with i exogenous, present value is a function of g_d and we may generally write $Y(g_d)$ for the present value function. This leaves it open to us to consider the characteristics of $Y(g_d)$ under different assumptions. In the present case, where

$$Y(g_d) = \frac{1}{i - g_d}$$

we have, as Fig. 6.3 illustrates, $dY/dg_d > 0$ and $d^2Y/dg_d^2 > 0$. If new

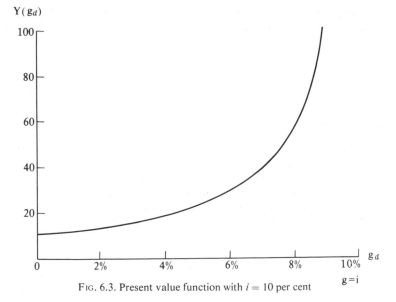

FIG. 6.3. Present value function with $i = 10$ per cent

share issues take place at a rate f, the growth rate of the dividend per share, g_d, is equal to the overall growth rate, g, less f:

$$g_d = g - f$$

The market value of the firm (M) is given by

$$M = \frac{Fd}{i - g + f} \qquad (6.1)$$

where F is the number of shares, Fd, is the total dividend payout and $1/(i - g + f)$ is the discount factor. Since Fd is the total dividend, (6.1) can also be written

$$M = \frac{Fd}{i - g + f} = \frac{(1 - r)\pi}{i - g + f} = \frac{(1 - r)pK}{i - g + f} \qquad (6.2)$$

where π = profit
 p = (reported) profit rate = π/K
and r = retention ratio.

The valuation ratio (v) is defined as the ratio of total market value to book value of assets. Thus

$$v = \frac{M}{K} \cdot \qquad (6.3)$$

But from (6.2)

$$M = \frac{(1 - r)pK}{i - g + f}$$

and so

$$v = \frac{(1 - r)p}{i - g + f} = \frac{p - rp}{i - g + f} \cdot \qquad (6.4)$$

If growth were all internally financed, a firm growing at rate g and with a profit rate (net of development expenditure) of p would have $g = rp$ and, for given g and p, a determinate retention ratio of

$$r = \frac{g}{p} \cdot \qquad (6.5)$$

However, in general the required retention ratio must take into account the contribution to funds of new issues. This contribution amounts to vf, assuming new shares are issued at the ruling market price. Thus

$$r = \frac{g - vf}{p} .$$ (6.6)

Substituting $g - vf$ for rp in (6.4) gives

$$v = \frac{p - g + vf}{i - g + f} .$$

Cross-multiplying yields

$$v = \frac{p - g}{i - g}$$ (6.7)

which is the general valuation formula.[15] One consequence of (6.7) is that, assuming certainty and full comprehension, the value of the firm for a given growth rate is independent of the method of finance. In that sense there is no optimal financial policy. This result is in accord with the well-known propositions of Modigliani and Miller,[16] although they do not really treat the problem in terms of a given growth rate. Another consequence is that method of finance does not set a limit to the growth rate. By the use of new issues the firm can grow no faster than if it uses internal finance only. This conclusion is also arrived at by J. H. Williamson.

Shareholders' welfare will be unaffected by a switch to internal financing for all expansion costs. Given that profits grow at the steady-state optimum g^* and that the funds to support this rate of growth have to be found (which is reasonable since g^* maximises profit), the existing shareholders will be indifferent to an increase in retentions because the loss in total payout will be matched by a fall in share issues (f). The rate at which new shareholders dilute old shareholders' claim on the payout thus falls, so that the expected earnings per existing shareholder will be unaffected. Conversely, if instead of financing a project out of profits the company pays out the money in dividends and sells shares to the same value, the value of the old shareholders' holdings are less but they have received cash instead. This can be reinvested at the same rate of return as that which the funds would have earned if employed by the firm in the first place.

In an imperfect world none of the above results necessarily follows. Shareholders will be affected by differential tax rates on dividends and capital gains; by the transaction costs of the reinvestment of accumulated dividends; and by uncertainty which may cause them to maintain a fixed level of investment in a company rather than allow their commitment to increase automatically as the firm grows. Management likewise will not be indifferent between retentions and new issues but will prefer the former. This preference can be formulated as a rise in the managerial cost of capital function:

> The cost of using internal funds for management-oriented firms is not the rate of return the stockholders can earn in the market but some much lower, totally subjective value set by the managers.[17]

Apart from the transaction costs of new issues, there is the likelihood that they will attract unwanted attention from the financial community to the policies the firm is pursuing. The growing firm will therefore have a rising marginal cost of capital. The constraint on managerial behaviour will arise not so much from a lack of funds as from a desire to finance internally investments with a rate of return lower than the shareholder opportunity cost of capital. Their disapproval lowers the firm's valuation.

Having shown that management will have nothing to gain by issuing shares instead of using internal finance, and that indeed it will prefer this method, we shall find it convenient to assume henceforth that all finance comes from retentions.

Another consequence of (6.7) is that, although unaffected by financial policy, the market value is affected by the growth rate and this places a real limitation on growth. This limit is p, the reported profit rate; that is, the rate of return after depreciation and the operating costs appropriate to the current level of output have been deducted. As g approaches p, i.e. as expansion costs take nearly all operating profit, the retention ratio would have to approach 100 per cent and the valuation ratio would approach zero. Since v cannot be negative, and indeed will not be permitted by shareholders to fall below a certain level as a result of too high a growth rate, it is clear where the real limitation on the supply of funds and on the growth rate occurs.

Retention/Dividend Policy

The proposition is that a firm which is maximising growth will pay out in dividends less than one which is maximising profit. This proposition will be investigated with the help of Fig. 6.4.

The curve $g(r\pi^*)$ shows the relationship between the retention ratio (r) and the growth rate (g) for a given level of profit (π). The level of profit assumed is in fact maximum profit (π^*), since a profit-maximising policy will maximise the flow of funds whether the intention is to use it to finance growth or to pay it out in dividends, increasing the value of the firm (M). $g(r\pi^*)$ is subject to diminishing returns because, although the amount of finance available increases directly with the retention ratio, rising marginal costs of expansion (either 'Penrose' costs or diversification costs) permit g to increase less than proportionately with r.

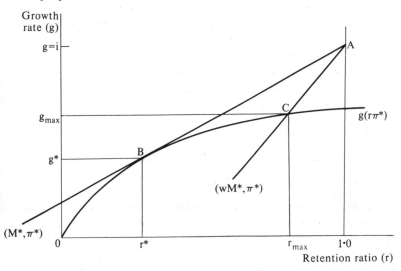

FIG. 6.4

AB and AC are iso-valuation curves. They show combinations of r and g which yield the same market valuation (M). Their positive slope implies that a reduction in dividends (increase in r) will have to be accompanied by an increase in the rate at which dividends are growing (g) if market disapproval is not to be expressed. Formally, the iso-valuation curves may be obtained from (6.2). Since there are no new issues, $f = 0$ and (6.2) becomes

$$M = \frac{(1 - r)\pi}{i - g} \qquad (6.8)$$

i.e. the present value of the stream of dividends ($(1 - r)\pi$). Rearrangement of (6.8) yields

$$g = i - \frac{(1 - r)\pi}{M}.$$

The iso-valuation curves are thus straight lines with a positive slope, converging on the point A where $r = 1$ and $g = i$. (If we retain our assumption that g is always less than i, the point will never actually be reached.) The highest iso-valuation curve consistent with $g(r\pi^*)$ is AB, since at B tangency occurs. The profit-maximising firm is thus in equilibrium at B: the profit-maximising retention ratio is r^* and the growth rate g^*. The tangency implies that the rate at which investors are prepared to trade dividends for capital gains is equal to the rate at which increments of capital can be transformed by the managerial team into a balanced growth of assets and output. The former rate is of course constant and equal to $(i - g)/(1 - r)$ (since $\partial g/\partial r = \pi/M$ where $M = [(1 - r)/(i - g)]\pi$.

However, a growth maximiser will presumably wish to push g beyond g^* by increasing r as far as capital-market vigilance will allow. The problem is formalised as follows:

$$\text{maximise} \quad g = g(r\pi^*)$$
$$\text{subject to} \quad M = wM^* \qquad 0 \leqslant w \leqslant 1$$
$$\pi = \pi(R).$$

w is J. H. Williamson's attempt to define the minimum level to which the value of the firm will be permitted to fall. It is the proportion of its potential maximum value (M^*) (i.e. that attained by a completely shareholder-oriented management) below which the management feels it could not safely allow the market value to fall. $\pi = \pi(R)$ means that current profit is related to current sales in the usual way (see Fig. 4.2). In Fig. 6.4 the iso-valuation curve AC is the locus of combinations of r and g yielding a value wM which is less than M. The growth maximiser will be in equilibrium at C, which yields the highest g consistent with $g(r\pi^*)$ and wM^*. Notice that the level of profit is still assumed to be π^*. The rate of growth is, however, higher ($g_{max} > g^*$) and the payout less ($r_{max} > r^*$). The only case in which both types of firm would have the same payout ratio is when $w = 1$, that is, when shareholders' displeasure is such, and their ability to exert pressure so great, that management must conform entirely and maximise M.

We can then summarise the argument so far as follows:

1. We are considering steady-state or balanced growth in the context of a rational capital market where there is no uncertainty.

2. A growth-maximising firm would produce the same current output as a profit-maximising firm, given the same capital stock (i.e. a growth maximiser maximises current profit).

3. A growth maximiser will grow faster than a profit maximiser by retaining a greater proportion of profits.

4. In principle growth is constrained by capital-market disapproval of too low a rate of return combined with too high a retention ratio, which reduces market valuation.

5. Given the assumptions, there is no optimal financial policy and internal financing can be assumed.

It is thus possible in principle to determine optimal values, according to the objectives of the firm, for market valuation, retention ratio, growth rate and profit rate; and consequently for static values such as current-period capital assets, output, sales revenue and profit. In principle, also, a further benefit arises in the opportunity to remove the arbitrary nature of the minimum profit constraint in the static Baumol model. The relationship between sales maximising and growth has not been investigated here, in spite of the fact that both Baumol and J. H. Williamson attempted to do so. It has been shown by Solow[18] that oversimplification invalidates the Williamson exercise and prevents us from drawing straight forward comparisons between the policies of growth maximisers, market-value maximisers and present-value-of-sales maximisers. However, it remains the case that whereas equilibrium in the static Baumol model was achieved through the setting of an arbitrary minimum level to total profit, a model where sales growth was the objective would generate automatically an appropriate current profit along with output and sales. Of course, except in the M-maximising case, our growth model is open to a similar charge of arbitrariness: we have achieved determinacy only by the use of the almost equally arbitrary coefficient of managerial insecurity, w.

NOTES AND REFERENCES

1. W. J. Baumol, 'On the Theory of Expansion of the Firm', *American Economic Review* (Dec. 1962). Reprinted in G. C. Archibald (ed.), *The Theory of the Firm* (Harmondsworth: Penguin Books 1971).

2. Galbraith, *The New Industrial State*, (London: Hamish Hamilton 1967).

3. Ibid., p. 172.

4. Meade, 'Is "The New Industrial State" Inevitable?' *Economic Journal* (June 1968) p. 387.

5. E. T. Penrose, *The Theory of the Growth of the Firm* (Oxford: Blackwell, 1959) p. 29.

6. G. M. Heal and S. Silberston, 'Alternative Managerial Objectives: An Explanatory Note', *Oxford Economic Papers* (July 1972) p. 137.

7. R. L. Marris and A. J. B. Wood (eds.), *The Corporate Economy*, (London: Macmillan 1971) p. xviii.

8. See H. G. Grabowski and D. C. Mueller, 'Managerial and Stockholder Welfare Models of Firm Expenditures', *Review of Economics and Statistics* (Feb. 1972).

9. *The Corporate Economy*, p. 8.

10. There may be economies of growth. The growing firm has some advantages over the stationary one. Because of increasing opportunities, it does better in attracting and holding good management. The capital stock of a growing firm will have a lower average age than that of firms of a stable or declining size. Thus the permanent-growth firm keeps the same capital–output ratio throughout by assumption, but because its capital stock is always newer it will probably be better. More negatively, large companies are subject to competitive pressures from rapidly growing newcomers who threaten established market positions. Thus growth becomes a prerequisite of survival – what Meade calls the Growth of the Profitable in an anology with Darwin's Survival of the Fittest. Firms with higher growth rates will therefore tend, up to a point, to have higher productivity and will be either more competitive on price and quality or more profitable. There is plenty of evidence of a positive association between changes in output and output per head in the industrial sector and also in retail and transport. According to K. D. George in his book *Industrial Organisation* (London: Allen & Unwin, 1972) pp. 26–30, the causal relationship could be either way: output growth may cause a rise in productivity or alternatively rises in productivity may cause falling costs and prices and therefore growth in output. Once the process is under way, cause and effect become indistinguishable through interaction: 'Either direction of causation is consistent with the behaviour of a firm operating under a goal structure in which growth is a significant factor.'

Nevertheless, for the most part the analysis which follows will assume, for the sake of simplicity, that the firm is always operating in the range of growth rates where efficiency is declining, that is, where the Penrose effect prevails.

11. For a firm with no static equilibrium an arbitrary initial output would have to be imposed. Obviously firms with the same growth rate but starting from a different size will always be of different size. The choice of initial size and the choice of an optimal rate would both in principle emerge from a more general model than is considered here. See R. M. Solow, 'Some Implications of Alternative Criteria for the Firm', in *The Corporate Economy*.

12. For justification of this assumption, see *The Corporate Economy*. Marris used a cross-section regression on 335 American corporations over the period 1950–63, finding the mean value of leverage to be about 20 per cent. The representative firm 'appeared to conform closely to a policy of long-run leverage stabilisation (as required for the steady-state model)'. The results imply a typical policy of financing two-thirds of asset expansion by retentions, with the rest divided about equally between 'steady' debt expansion (i.e. expansion proportionate to total assets expansion) and new stock issues (ibid., p. 424).

13. In general, with continuous compounding and discounting, the sequence will be

$$d + de^{g-i} + de^{2(g-i)} + \cdots + de^{t(g-i)}$$

If the present value of a member of the series t years hence is $de^{t(g-i)}$, the series will converge as long as $i > g$. The integral sum of the infinite series is

$$d \int_0^\infty e^{t(g-i)} \, dt = d \left[\frac{e^{t(g-i)}}{(g-i)} \right]_0^\infty$$

$$= d \left[\frac{e^{\infty(g-i)}}{(g-i)} - \frac{e^{0(g-i)}}{(g-i)} \right].$$

The first bracketed term approaches zero and

$$e^{0(g-i)} = 1.$$

Thus the sum approaches

$$d \left(-\frac{1}{g-i} \right) = \frac{d}{i-g}.$$

Similarly, in the case of a constant dividend the integral sum would be

$$d \int_0^\infty e^{-it} \, dt$$

and the sum would approach d/i.

Notice that, when the discounting takes place once a year, as was assumed on p. 94 above, if the first term is d, rather than $d/(1 + i)$, the sum to infinity is $d(1 + i)/i$, rather than d/i, a difference, not surprisingly, of d.

14. For a lengthy discussion of this point, see *Managerial Capitalism*, Chap. 5.

15. (6.7) supersedes the valuation expression in *Managerial Capitalism*, which is

$$v = \frac{1-r}{i/p - r} = \frac{1-r}{1-r+n}$$

where $n = (k - p)/p$ is the 'negative return discrepancy ratio' – a measure of the extent to which the firm's policies are unprofitable. The emphasis is thus on the choice of an appropriate retention ratio, whereas in *The Corporate Economy*, using the 'Kahn' formula, the decision about retentions is subsumed in the decision about the growth rate. Marris attributes the difference in the expressions for v to a failure to assume consistent comprehension by the stock market: 'I assumed that the market fully comprehended the implications of retentions, but only partly comprehended the implications of new issues' (*The Corporate Economy*, p. 23).

16. F. Modigliani and M. Miller, 'The Cost of Capital, Corporation Finance and the Theory of Investment', *American Economic Review* (June 1958).

17. Grabowski and Mueller, op. cit.

18. Solow, 'Some Implications of Alternative Criteria for the Firm', in *The Corporate Economy*.

7

TAKE-OVER, MANAGERIAL UTILITY AND GROWTH

THE treatment of the Marris model in this chapter is based on the original version in *The Economic Theory of 'Managerial' Capitalism*, but draws also upon Marris's contribution to *The Corporate Economy*, where considerable simplification and amendment is carried out.

In the last chapter it was established that the constraints on growth arose out of market disapproval of falling rates of return. J. H. Williamson's proposition was that wM^* represented a lower limit on the total market valuation of the firm. There are various ways in which market valuation might influence managerial behaviour and some of them will be mentioned later in this chapter. In the first chapter of *Managerial Capitalism* Marris developed a take-over model through which it was possible to define a minimum safe valuation ratio and consequently to derive a maximum balanced rate of growth consistent with it.

As a preliminary to a theory of take-over the following assumptions should be made explicit:

(*a*) Investors are aware of the policies which all quoted companies are going to pursue and know the rates of return these will produce.

(*b*) Policies, once decided, will not be changed. Thus, for example, whatever the existing rate of return before a new asset expansion, the average rate of return after expansion has taken place will asymptotically approach the marginal rate − that is, the rate of return expected on the 'new' project − because the new policy on rate of return and retentions will continue indefinitely.[1]

(*c*) In the absence of discriminatory taxes and transaction costs, shareholders are indifferent between income and capital gain because the only source of capital gain is rising dividends which are perfectly forecastable in view of the constant financial policies being pursued.

(*d*) Financial policy consists of the choice of an appropriate retention ratio. Growth by retentions is always possible and is a 'process with which the market is powerless to interfere except by enforcing a change of management or by shaming management through low prices'.[2]

TAKE-OVER

If one accepts the evidence given in Chapter 1 of shareholder inability to exert on management collective pressure sufficient to cause a deviation in policy, one is left with the proposition that the only effective action they can take is to sell their shares to a raider who can use the votes acquired to remove the offending management. Marris defines a raider as

> a person or company aiming for virtual ownership. He or they intend to acquire sufficient stock to be able to dismiss and appoint directors at will, to distribute capital, to amalgamate with other firms controlled, perhaps, by themselves. . . . They may plan to reorganise the firm, sell the assets, distribute capital and realise quick capital gains. Alternatively, they may intend to continue the business on existing lines, but managed with greater efficiency or with a different pay-out policy.[3]

The problem is to determine what policies existing management can pursue to avoid this danger. In the formulation of a policy the management has complete control over the retention ratio but none over the discount rate. In principle the rate of return is within their control but is an endogenous rather than a decision variable. Given the firm's innate efficiency, a policy may therefore be characterised by the values chosen for r and p, determining g; or for g and p, determining r. The valuation formula derived in the last chapter ($v = (p - g)/(i - g)$) emphasises the latter: a policy consists of a choice of growth rate, hence a retention ratio, hence a valuation ratio.

The lower limit of the valuation ratio is given by the safety condition

$$v_{im} > v_{ij} \qquad (7.1)$$

where v_{im} is defined as the market valuation ratio of the ith firm, given the existing management's policies on p and g. v_{ij} is the valuation set by j, the most dangerous raider, who is the raider with the highest valuation ratio for i, based on the policy he would pursue if successful. The safety condition (7.1) thus says that firm i is likely to be raided if the raider who values i most values it more highly than the market does. This concept of safety may be compared with J. H. Williamson's definition in terms of the highest valuation attainable by a shareholder-oriented management. In the Marris version, however, we may say that j will be less dangerous the more 'managerial' he is.

In fact, although neoclassical apologists of profit maximising would wish to identify the raider threat as one of the competitive-equilibrium-generating fingers of the Hidden Hand, powerful arguments can be advanced for the relative security of incumbent managements:

1. There is little reason to suggest that the rate of return which could be achieved by raiders will be greater than that achieved by the existing management. Although the latter is intent on pursuing unprofitable growth and has depressed the rate of return below the discount rate, it is likely that the best policy that potential alternative managements would be able to offer would be similarly unprofitable. This may not be so, of course, if existing management is characterised by inefficiency (low p) rather than (or as well as) by a conscience which is insufficiently shareholder-oriented (high g, hence high r). But there is in fact little empirical evidence (as was seen in Chapter 1) that profitability increases after take-over (see above, p. 11).

2. Raiders tend to be scarce in relation to their efficiency: those with the highest potential profit rate for the 'victim' will tend to be those with the highest discount rate, reflecting a high alternative rate of return on the assets already under their control.

3. Most reassuring of all for incumbents: j's finance supply curve will be less than perfectly elastic. The supply price of funds – the rate at which j discounts the potential profits from i – will increase with the sum required for acquisition of i. Bigger firms are therefore in less danger of being taken over. The significant feature of modern capitalism is the skewed size-distribution which ensures that even if firms of average size were subject to

the constraints provided by the threat of take-over, 'the giants who produce the bulk of the output would remain relatively immune'.[4]

DEMAND GROWTH

Growth in the Marris model, as in the others we have considered, is balanced or sustainable growth: that is, 'growth which is consistent with the firm's continuing on a financial basis such that the same rate can be maintained indefinitely'.[5] If, for example, assets were to expand more rapidly than the volume of saleable output, average use of capacity would gradually decline, reducing the rate of return on capital – which is not consistent with a constant growth rate. If assets expanded less rapidly than output, the capital-output ratio would fall until the required output increases were unobtainable.

The theory of demand advanced by Marris is a significant departure from the classical approach and deserves at least as much attention as his theory of the capital market or of managerial objectives. However, it is here possible to attempt only a brief outline from which it is hoped the flavour of Marris's contribution emerges – but not an account of the specific and detailed functional relationships which he presents. The reader is urged to grapple for himself with chap. 4 of *Managerial Capitalism*.

The theory emphasises the role of diversification in the dynamics of growth. Growth by diversification may be of two kinds – 'differentiated' or 'imitative'. In the former case the products are new to the firm and to the public whereas in the latter case they are new only to the firm. The effects of the successful introduction of a differentiated product are spread thinly over demand for products as a whole and are imperceptible to the producers of any one existing product. The effects of an imitative product are, in contrast, felt by a small number of other firms. Many products will of course contain elements of both differentiation and imitation at the same time, but in principle the types are separable.

Growth by Differentiation

The inadequacy of the Marshallian demand curve – a static, stable, reversible dependence of quantity on prices and income – is two fold:

1. It assumes that the consumer has a relatively stable and comprehensive preference system.

2. It assumes that the preferences of individuals are independent: that one person's decision to buy a given product will not have been affected by other people's decisions – or at least that any effect will be negligible.

In fact wants are neither static, stable nor reversible but are the product of experience, so that each act of consumption permanently alters the consumer. A repetition of the same situation would elicit a different response. Therefore instead of defining the primary economic goal as the satisfaction of existing wants, it should perhaps be defined as the discovery and refinement of new wants. Most people are searching for new experiences. Furthermore, the experiences which produce wants are not always direct: wants can also result from vicarious experience.

The distinction made between wants and needs is useful:

A product meets a need if it provides the consumer with sensible advantages in the achievement of specific socio-economic aims. But consumers cannot 'want' the product until they have experienced it in action, until in fact it has been created and is in use. When they do come to want it, they also need it. Before this, the need can be described as latent. There is a latent need for a product if, were it created, it would become wanted. The commercial process consists of sensing the existence of latent needs and exploiting them, i.e. converting them into conscious wants by marketing and advertising appropriate products[6] (p. 139).

For the purpose of the want-creating process, two types of consumer are distinguished:

1. Pioneers – individuals or families who buy new products without stimulus from others.
2. Sheep – the general run of consumers.

In both types wants are established by consumption experience, but with sheep they must first be planted in the mind by another person. It is assumed that pioneers are 'stochastic events distributed among the whole population of sheep': in other words, in the absence of special knowledge about a consumer he is as likely to be a pioneer as any other consumer. When a new product is introduced the immediate consumers are a small number of pioneers. Their purchases eventually flatten out but not before they have begun a chain reaction by stimulating their contacts. The beginning of the reaction depends on the number of pioneers reaching some definite critical size. In an extreme case criticality may occur almost as soon as the product appears, and with few pioneers. In the general case the number of pioneers required will represent a significant proportion of the market population.

In order to stimulate each other consumers must be in socio-economic contact, a state which is correlated with social class and with income, although not completely so. 'We cannot say for certain that either shared social class or shared income class is an exclusive ingredient in a socio-economic contact.' Its definition is therefore un-avoidably circular: a socio-economic contact is a person with whom one has a relationship such that his consumption behaviour is capable of influencing one's own. A *primary group* is a group of consumers all of whom are in socio-economic contact. One primary group will probably intersect others; that is, an individual may belong to more than one group (then two groups are 'linked' in degree *n* if their intersection contains at least *n* persons). The chance of obtaining a chain reaction clearly depends on the structure of the system of groups and links.

A simple geographical type of socio-economic structure is the linear suburb illustrated in Fig. 7.1. The dots represent families, the broken

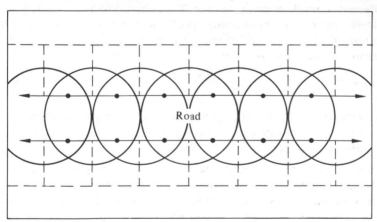

Fig. 7.1

lines garden fences and the circles enclose primary groups. Each family is in contact only with neighbours on either side and the three families opposite. Each thus has five contacts and belongs to two primary groups, but the primary groups themselves each contain only four elements. Each primary group has two 2-unit intersections with adjacent groups; that is, it is linked in the second degree with the groups either side of it.

However, the presence to a significant extent of social barriers (or more trivial 'bars') causes primary groups to be irregularly shaped and variable in size and the chains of linked groups to be interrupted. Thus the market population will be divided into a considerable number of distinct sets called *secondary groups*. Any unbroken chain of n-degree linked primary groups is a secondary group of degree n. Typical causes of breaks in the chain and thus of *stratification* are physical factors such as housing layout and highways and of course income and class barriers. The basic problem for the firm is that, whatever the nature of the break in the chain, in order to achieve a total saturation of the market it must get a chain reaction going on each side of the break.

New products will pass through three stages: gestation, explosion and saturation, where explosion is defined as an unstable process of change from gestation to saturation. A secondary group becomes critical when the probability of explosion ($P(E_i)$) is unity, and this occurs when the ratio of the total number of pioneers obtained in a secondary group to the total number of consumers in that group is p_i, the *critical ratio*. Formulae for both $P(E_i)$ and p_i are derived in terms of the threshold number of contacts for the product, the number of consumers per primary group, the number of consumers in the primary population, the number of primary groups, the number of secondary groups, and the number of links between one group and another. In economic terms the critical ratio is a measure of the relative cost of obtaining a market in terms of pioneers, and it is likely that a considerable part of the development costs of a new product are those associated with the process of obtaining pioneers: 'Our theory indicates that the cost per unit of ultimate sales is governed by a precise formula in which the unit cost declines with scale'[7] (p. 170).

Diversification into a succession of large markets will therefore yield a higher rate of return than diversification into small markets. No conflict thus arises in this area between profit maximisation and volume maximisation. However, it is possible that, after products have reached the saturation stage, the firm will have to resolve a conflict between volume and profit by virtue of its pricing policy: either low price yielding high sales and lower profit, or a higher price, lower sales and maximum profit. Marris claims that the conflict will in fact rarely be experienced because demand is usually so inelastic after saturation that prices below profit-maximising price would produce only small increases in volume and large reductions in profit. It can be assumed that 'saturated sales volumes are little smaller than the maxima consistent with earning any profit at all'. The optimum gestation price will normally be higher than the optimum saturation price.

As far as differentiated growth is concerned, then, the general relationship between growth and profitability can be described. The profitability of a product over its whole history – through gestation, explosion and saturation – consists of an early rise, followed by flattening and gradual decline. Therefore the higher the proportion of young products in the catalogue at any given time, the higher the average profit rate, since as each successful newcomer is launched it establishes a temporarily dominant position in its market. However, this beneficial effect of an increase in the diversification rate must be set against the harmful effect of 'declining intrinsic utility' – declining consumer appeal – over the range of new products launched by a given firm in a given period:

> The stock of exploitable needs latent among consumers at any one time cannot but be limited and so also must be the capacity of any one managerial organisation to perceive them. The further the inventive resources of a firm are stretched within a given period the less useful are likely to be the results. In other words we must postulate that the new products launched by a given firm in a given period are subject to declining intrinsic utility (p. 182).

Thus the average index of profitability among new products eventually falls 'until a point is reached where marginal products are so devoid of merit that the expenditure required for success becomes virtually infinite'.

Growth by Imitation

In considering diversification through marketing products which will be in direct competition with existing products we may distinguish two cases:

(a) entry into exploding markets; and
(b) entry into static markets.

Marris calls method (*a*) – a popular method of growth – 'bandwaggoning'. The advantages are that no innovation is required, much of the uncertainty of the outcome is removed and the chain reaction has already been begun by the firm which was first in the field. The tension between competitors in an expanding market is less than in a static market and there is likely to be a range of responses from retaliation to co-operation, with the latter 'especially plausible': 'Business communities, like many animal societies, develop many ethical restraints against fighting to the death, transgression of which may invite the costs of commercial ostracism' (p. 189). The defender will be unlikely to retaliate in the early stages, owing to uncertainty about how fast the market is expanding and about the price policies the invaders will pursue, and to the fact that his own sales are still growing. In some cases retaliation will not be necessary because 'the imitator, once he has established a reasonable share in the market, may anticipate retaliation and raise his price before it happens: peace breaks out before incipient war becomes open'. There are thus generally two phases: at first price is any price markedly below the enemy price and sales are growing rapidly; in the second phase price is the 'peace price' and sales grow at the explosion rate of the market as a whole.

With method (*b*) – imitative growth in static markets – the conflict is intense and the problem may be characterised by an actual or potential game of economic survival. Marris discusses the economic applicability of two-person zero-sum games such as 'gambler's ruin' and concludes that the implications for the demand-growth function of imitative strategies are similar to those for differentiated strategies.

Given the optimal amount of bandwaggoning in the sphere of imitative diversification, the firm is thus faced with a policy decision as to how much weight to give to imitative as opposed to differentiated growth. One would expect an emphasis on imitation in firms which were weak in imagination but clever in production.

The Growth–Profitability Function

The implication of the preceding section is that the steady profit rate is a function of the steady growth rate. A zero growth rate would be associated with a small positive profit rate arising from a constant catalogue of saturated products, for which a zero autonomous trend in demand is assumed. As the growth rate increases the profit rate rises, reflecting temporary monopoly in successful new products. At the same time the stimulus to managerial efficiency provided by growth (a reverse Penrose effect) causes the capital–output ratio to fall. In principle a firm could be in equilibrium on a rising part of its growth–profitability function: if it could safely increase the rate of growth it could increase the rate of profit also, but it cannot grow faster because the rate of profit, although rising, is not rising fast enough for the market to approve of the necessary fund-raising increase in retentions. However, although Marris argued in *Managerial Capitalism* that this relationship was reasonable, he excluded it in the later version to be found in *The Corporate Economy*, on the ground that it constitutes an unnecessary complication. It is this later version which will be followed here: we therefore assume that the growth–profitability function has negative first and negative second derivatives over the whole range.

THE VALUATION CURVE

The valuation expression $(p - g)/(i - g)$ can now be written

$$v = v(g) = \frac{p(g) - g}{i - g}$$

where $p(g)$ is the growth–profitability function. $v(g)$ is the growth–valuation function or valuation curve. Alternatively, we may write

$$v = v(g) = D(g) \cdot Y(g)$$

where $D(g) = p(g) - g$ is a general dividend function (remembering that $g = rp$) and $Y(g) = 1/(i - g)$ is, as we saw on p. 95 above, the present value function.

The shape of $v(g)$ depends on the characteristics of $D(g)$ and $Y(g)$. Since $dD/dg = dp/dg - 1$, and given that dp/dg is always negative, it follows that dD/dg is always negative. $dY/dg = 1/(i - g)^2$ is always positive, as Fig. 6.3 showed, because the faster the dividend is expected to grow the greater the value of the share. Thus

$$dv/dg = dD/dg \cdot Y(g) + dY/dg \cdot D(g)$$

which may be either positive or negative. The valuation curve may therefore have a positive maximum with respect to g, as in Fig. 7.2. Alternatively, dv/dg may be negative throughout.

The valuation curve gives the best obtainable valuation ratio for a given growth rate, taking into account variations in the rate of return and the retention ratio, and assuming that optimal decisions on diversification and its associated policy matters are made. It is an important and useful analytical device because it incorporates concepts and information which both shareholders and managers find highly significant:

1. From the point of view of shareholders v is presumably the main element in their welfare. The value given at a particular point on the curve is the stock market's reaction to those aspects of the firm's situation which are relevant to investors. The classical solution – maximising shareholder welfare – is obviously at A in Fig. 7.2.

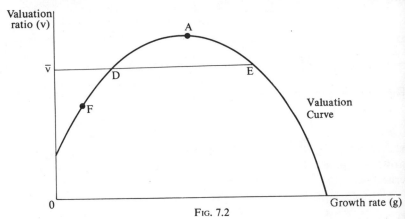

FIG. 7.2

2. From the point of view of managers the valuation curve can be applied in two ways:
   (a) It enables a general formulation of the growth-maximising model subject to a security constraint. In Fig. 7.2 the intersection of the horizontal at $v = \bar{v}$ with the valuation curve at E indicates the maximum safe growth rate. The intersection at D implies that there is also a minimum safe rate of growth: thus a firm at F would have to grow faster in order to survive. $\bar{v}$ is determined either by Williamson's wM^* or by Marris's v_{ij}.

(b) The valuation curve can be viewed as the constraint or transformation curve subject to which managerial utility may be maximised.

A MANAGERIAL UTILITY FUNCTION

The suggested function is

$$U = U(g, v) \tag{7.2}$$

where g stands for the satisfactions derived from power, prestige and salary and v stands for the related but different satisfactions of security from take-over on the one hand and of stock-market approval on the other.

1. Psychological and sociological motives are satisfied in this simplified function. An individual may partly satisfy dynamic aspirations by rising within one firm or by successive inter-firm transfers; but as he approaches the top he can progress further only by inducing the firm itself to grow. The motive for collective expansion may be directly founded in personal ambition. In addition, growth is an index of professional competence: 'To be judged a good businessman normally means not that he has a nose for profits but that he is a good organiser.'[8] There is thus a constant urge to do something new and creative. But since large corporations are bureaucratic the emphasis is not so much on the character of the goods produced but rather on the skill with which activities are organised. On the other hand, there are positive utilities associated with v. It is not merely that by adhering to a minimum v the managers avoid the sanction of take-over. Values of v greater than $\bar{v}$ will be desired to the extent that managers identify with shareholders or derive satisfaction from stock-market approval. The likelihood of such identification was discussed in Chapter 1.

2. Economic motives are satisfied by bonuses of various types, by stock option schemes and, most important, by basic compensation or salary:

   (a) Almost all bonus schemes are in fact scale-dependent, probably because managers so devise them.

   (*b*) Stock option schemes on their current scale hardly ensure
      profit maximising, in Marris's view, although they do
      significantly reinforce the incentive to maintain a reasonable
      level of *v*. As we saw in Chapter 1, the evidence on
      managerial share ownership is somewhat conflicting (see
      above, p. 31).

   (*c*) Salaries are not correlated with profits[9] but with growth
      because large firms have more high-level posts and because
      there is little high-level mobility among managers, who are
      inelastic in supply, determine their own salaries and are more
      productive in their present teams than they would be
      elsewhere.

Thus *g* and *v* emerge as appropriate proxy variables for the motives of
managers: power, prestige and salary on the one hand, and security
plus stock-market approval on the other. Positive marginal utilities
will normally be associated with both so that they will be competing
sources of managerial satisfaction.

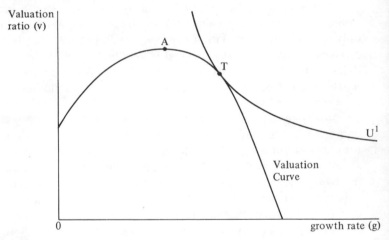

Fig. 7.3

   In Fig. 7.3, U^1 is one of an infinite number of managerial
indifference curves. They are negatively sloped wherever the assumption holds that both growth and security yield positive marginal utility.
They are convex to the origin provided marginal utility diminishes.
Constrained maximum utility occurs at *T* where the valuation curve is
tangent to the highest possible indifference curve U^1.

If no utility attaches to growth the indifference curves become horizontal and the result would be a solution at A where market valuation is maximised. This outcome is made more likely if, as v falls, it reaches a level at which the probability of take-over becomes $1 \cdot 0$. At that level all indifference curves, whatever their slope elsewhere, become horizontal. If the tangency occurs at A we have the long-run neoclassical equilibrium where the only safe strategy is to maximise profit because only those who do so survive. Neoclassical profit maximising would in this way emerge as a special case of the general managerial model in which, although managerial objectives were in principle viable (and therefore g remained as an argument in U), in practice it emerged that opportunities for pursuit of growth at the expense of profit did not arise when either the product-market conditions or the capital-market conditions were competitive.

If, as in Fig. 7.3, tangency occurs at a point where the valuation curve has a negative slope, two conclusions emerge:

1. Utility maximisation for managers involves a faster growth rate than would utility maximisation for owners. It also involves a lower profit rate;[10] but since the rate of return is rising at the point of maximum valuation it is possible that it is still rising or at its maximum at that rate of growth which managers desire.
2. Firms in growth industries — that is, industries where the growth–profitability curve, and therefore the valuation curve, are shifted outwards as compared with other industries — should give evidence of higher profit rates and valuation ratios as well as higher growth rates. (The tangency at T would be likely to move in a north-easterly direction.)

Marris has suggested[11] that the model may be more precisely specified. Formally, the problem is

$$\text{maximise} \quad U = U(g, v)$$

$$\text{subject to} \quad v = v(g) = D(g) \cdot Y(g)$$

The idea is that it would be highly convenient if the basic functions of the constraint — the dividend function and the present value function — were linear. If this were the case the $v(g)$ function, being quadratic, would describe a straightforward parabola. Demand growth, as we have seen, requires search, research, development and marketing expenditures. These may be normalised by the book value of assets.

We have assumed that p was ultimately a declining function of demand growth due to dynamic diminishing returns. We now simplify by assuming that development expenditure is a linear function of growth so that a constant proportionate outlay would produce a constant growth rate. We also assume that the Penrose effect does not operate so as to yield managerial diseconomies of growth. Then

$$\frac{G}{K} = a(g - \bar{g}).$$

G/K is normalised development expenditure; g is the desired growth rate; $\bar{g}$ is the immanent growth rate, i.e. the growth rate if the firm incurred no development expenditure. The coefficient a is therefore a constant measuring the marginal cost of growth – independent both of the passage of time and of the value of g. This is the basic linearising assumption.

The dividend function is, of course, for a given growth rate,

$$D(g) = p - rp = p - g$$

where p is the reported profit rate. But $p = \bar{p} - G/K$, where $\bar{p}$ is the operating profit rate, that is, the rate that would be earned if the firm behaved as if immanent. Thus the dividend function is

$$D(g) = \bar{p} - ag + a\bar{g} - g$$
$$= \bar{p} + a\bar{g} - (1 + a)g.$$

In order to justify a linear present value function Marris relies on the proposition that with uncertainty increasing with futurity the present value will increase with the expected growth rate but will always be finite. In fact $Y(g_d)$ clearly cannot in practice take on the characteristics it has in Fig. 6.3. Whether the rise in the discount rate, as growth increases and as payments become more future, can be expected to counteract the rise in g, so as to make Y linear, is obviously debatable and in principle testable. The function suggested is

$$Y(g) = y_1 + y_2 g$$

where the coefficients y_1 and y_2 arise from the degree of risk-aversion, the riskless discount rate and the rate at which uncertainty increases with futurity.

The growth–valuation function is then

$$v = [(p + a\bar{g} - g(1 + a)](y_1 + y_2 g)$$

which is the equation of a parabola with a finite positive maximum.

The classical growth rate, obtained by setting $\partial v/\partial g = 0$, is

$$g^* = \tfrac{1}{2}\left(\frac{\bar{p} + a\bar{g}}{1 + a}\right) - \tfrac{1}{2}\frac{y_1}{y_2} \ .$$

The classical growth rate is therefore a linear function of the operating profit rate and the immanent growth rate. It should thus be relatively simple to test an assumption of classical behaviour in this model: the slope of the g^* function, in terms of operating profit rate, is $\tfrac{1}{2}/(1 + a)$ where a is the cost of growth; the constant term is equal to half the stock market's growth-aversion ratio, y_1/y_2. Since the operating profit rate $(\bar{p})$ is difficult to observe, the growth rate could be regressed on p, the reported profit rate, since $p = \bar{p} - a(g - \bar{g})$.

However, whereas $v(g)$, in this form, is convenient for maximising v, it does not yield such a simple solution to the 'managerial' problem of maximising g subject to a constraint on v. Marris does not present the result but does describe the characteristics of the solution. The managerial growth rate is equal to g^* plus a number which is always positive (except for the limiting case where it is zero) and which increases with $\bar{p}$; but the relationship is not linear.

Marris does suggest an alternative linear model which has the advantage that it produces a linear managerial growth-rate function, but the disadvantage that, because v is throughout a decreasing function of g, it predicts zero growth always for the classical solution.

Empirical evidence strongly supporting or refuting the hypotheses implicit in the models outlined here is not available. The methodological problems are so acute that correlation coefficients tend to be too small and their direction too inconsistent for there to be more than the most tentative expressions of opinion. The relationship expected, for example, between growth and profitability would depend on whether firms in the sample could be assumed to be on their demand-growth curves (or whether allowance should be made for X-inefficiency); and whether they could be assumed, on a managerial hypothesis, to be on a demand–growth function of the type postulated (or whether allowance should be made for some firms to be on the rising portion of such a function). Tests which discriminate between neoclassical and managerial predictions are therefore difficult to devise.

Marris cites the evidence of M. Gordon and of Meyer and Kuh.[12] who produced correlation coefficients between retention ratio and growth rate, between growth rate and rate of return and between retention ratio and rate of return. The results are complex and inconclusive, but Marris considers them 'rather damaging for anyone who wants to believe that firms actually behave neoclassically'.[13]

There is a good deal of evidence of a positive relationship between profitability and growth. This evidence does not discriminate between alternative theories since they would all predict such a relationship. All such evidence does is to confirm a relationship which might tend to become obscured by other factors such as differences in the quality and goals of managers, the degree of market competition and the growth of aggregate or industry demand; Singh and Whittington found[14] a 'fairly strong association' between growth and profitability, with the latter explaining about 50 per cent of the variation in growth rates and other factors (such as those just mentioned) explaining the rest. However, neither productivity nor profitability was found to be significantly related to the size of the firm. Average profitability was inversely related to size but not to a statistically significant extent. But the dispersion of profit rates was significantly less for large firms than for small. One explanation would be that large firms are more diversified but less adventurous and so avoid loss but neglect opportunities for unusually large gain. Radice[15] found a negative relation between size and rate of profit and a positive relation between growth and profit which agree with the Singh and Whittington results. None of this really supports the hypothesis that managers with a sales or growth goal will pursue their objectives to the point of sacrificing profit.

The statistical relationship between growth rates and rates of return is what one would expect. It helps explain, if explanation were needed, the heavily skewed distribution of firms by size, which is such a prominent feature of advanced industrial economies. The absolute amount by which a large firm can grow in a given period is greater than for a small firm – even though they may grow at the same proportionate rate. This is because the larger firm has greater assets to begin with, has an entrenched position with consumers and suppliers, and can obtain finance more easily, whether internally or externally. This might well cause it to grow at a faster rate than the small firm, but even if the growth rates were the same the result would be an increasing absolute gap between the large and the small.[16]

Radice classified firms into owner-controlled and management-controlled on a similar basis to that used by Sargant Florence.[17] It was found that although owner-controlled firms have higher rates of profit than management-controlled firms, they also have higher growth rates. Owner-controlled firms do not, on this evidence, show a greater tendency to maximise profit. It is suggested, though, that because the sample consisted of very large firms, the control that owners were able to exert at board level was frustrated by Marris-type managers lower down. The study also suggested that the dependence of large firms on the capital market may be greater than is sometimes supposed, and opportunity for managerial discretion correspondingly less: rapidly growing firms tended to finance some 45 per cent of assets expansion externally.

A recent study by Whittington[18] attempts to discover to what extent, if any, the process of raising finance through the market leads to a more efficient use of funds, in terms of profitability, than internal financing. The basic data were the published accounts of 1,955 companies which were engaged in manufacturing and distribution and which were in continuous independent existence throughout the period 1948–60. Whittington introduces as extra explanatory variables the past profitability and growth of the companies concerned. Both variables would have significant influence on future profitability, and if omitted would impart unwanted bias to the result. The effect of their inclusion is to isolate the independent impact of external financing on future profitability in firms having equal past profitability and growth. For a similar reason the analysis pays separate attention to firms whose past profitability was below the average for all firms. The justification for this is that a firm with a high rate of return in the past would have to lower its future rate of return in order to push investment to the profit-maximising point where marginal profitability was zero.[19] In this case the discipline of the stock market would necessarily be reflected in higher profitability only among firms whose past profitability was below average. Taking these factors into account, the result obtained is that the average future profitability of externally financed firms is 1·91 percentage points higher than that of otherwise similar firms which relied on internal finance. This effect is characterised as 'definite but rather small'; the extent of the effect does not, according to Whittington, depend on the amount of new finance raised. The fact of raising external finance is more important than the amount raised. The conclusion is that 'the profitability of firms might be improved if more firms had resort to the capital market, but not if the firms which already have resort to the market raised larger amounts'.

Some evidence on take-over was introduced in Chapter 1 (pp. 9–12 above). However, Singh[20] has observed that the Marris theory of take-over is not easily testable, since although v_{im} is empirically measurable, v_{ij} cannot be observed. On the other hand, Singh considers that the idea of the threat of take-over (the constraint on v), as embodied in the Marris growth model (see Fig. 7.2), has richer empirical content. It should be possible to test either the hypothesis that unless a firm achieves a certain minimum valuation it is almost certain to be acquired or, less strongly, the hypothesis that the higher the valuation ratio the lower the probability that the firm will be taken over. Unfortunately Singh's evidence refutes the stronger hypothesis: although the valuation ratio of taken-over firms is significantly less than that of non-taken-over firms, a relatively large number of acquired firms have above-average valuation ratios and a similar proportion of non-taken-over firms have below-average ratios. The evidence also suggests that

> the inverse relationship between the valuation ratio and the probability of take-over is likely to be very weak. Thus the achievement of a relatively high valuation ratio, far from guaranteeing a firm against take-over, may not even greatly reduce its chance of being acquired.[21]

However, D. A. Kuehn,[22] in a study of 1961 data for United Kingdom companies, found that the valuation ratio was a significant determinant of the probability of take-over. A stratified sample of 250 firms classified as 'industrial and commercial' had a mean valuation ratio of approximately 1, as expected. 51 of the firms had probably experienced a take-over bid, of which 38 were successful (identification of unsuccessful attempts may be incomplete). Although v in itself had low explanatory power – which is to be expected because of cross-sectional sampling – it is suggested that whatever the objective probability of take-over based on historical occurrence of the event, managers may associate a much higher subjective probability of take-over with a given valuation ratio because of the regret attached to being taken over. Furthermore, if they regard the other objective influences as random, unknown or unalterable they may see their security as dependent on the one variable they do have the power to influence – the valuation ratio.

NOTES AND REFERENCES

1. One practical objection to this is that it implies that new capital will be used in an identifiable set of new projects with an identifiable rate of return different from that on the rest of the company's assets. This could happen (for example in the case of North Sea oil) but it would not normally be discernible by investors.

2. *The Economic Theory of 'Managerial' Capitalism* p. 27.

3. Ibid., p. 29.

4. Ibid., p. 40. The distinction between the giant firm and the large firm is made by O. E. Williamson (see note 34 of Chapter 1).

5. Ibid., p. 118.

6. All this by no means renders the Marshallian concept redundant. The static demand curve is an analytical device: it does not imply that wants are static − merely that there are situations in which they may be sufficiently stable for equilibrium to be reached before everything changes. Marshall was quite aware of the complexity and of the changing and dynamic character of wants: 'Human wants and desires are countless in number and very various in kind ... |man| desires not merely larger quantities of the things he has been accustomed to consume, but better qualities of those things; he desires a greater choice of things, and things that will satisfy new wants growing up in him.' (*Principles of Economics*, bk III. p. 73.)

7. *Managerial Capitalism*, p. 170.

8. Ibid., p. 58.

9. See D. R. Roberts, *Executive Compensation* (New York: Free Press 1959).

10. If we had allowed $p(g)$ to increase at first with g we should now have to say that 'managerial' growth could lead to a higher rate of profit than 'capitalist' growth. Thus where $p(g)$ does have a positive maximum, as is assumed in *Managerial Capitalism*, the rate of growth which maximises profitability can never also maximise the valuation ratio. The peak of the $v(g)$ curve must occur at a smaller rate of growth than the peak of the $p(g)$ curve: as one approaches the peak of the $p(g)$ curve, g is increasing rapidly and p hardly at all. This entails large increases in r and therefore in the discount rate (no longer exogenous) which at least cause v to increase less rapidly. At the peak of the $p(g)$ curve, p is constant and g increasing: v must therefore already be falling at this point. The tangency at T could therefore happen before or at maximum p. Of course, so far we have assumed that increases in the discount rate do not take place and that $Y(g)$ increases exponentially. In his 'linear' model (above p. 118) Marris argues that increases in i will 'straighten out' $v(g)$.

11. *The Corporate Economy*, p. 304.

12. M. Gordon, *The Investment, Financing and Valuation of the Corporation* (Homewood, Ill.: Irwin, 1962); J. Meyer and E. Kuh, *The Investment Decision* (Cambridge, Mass.: Harvard Univ. Press, 1957).

13. *Managerial Capitalism*, p. 287.

14. A. Singh and G. Whittington, *Growth, Profitability and Valuation* (Cambridge Univ. Press, 1968).

15. H. K. Radice, 'Control Type, Profitability and Growth in Large Firms: An Empirical Study', *Economic Journal* (Sept. 1971).

16. An interesting attempt at providing a non-economic explanation for the skewed size-distribution is the so-called Law of Proportionate Effect or Gibrat's Law (R. Gibrat, *Les Inégalités Economiques*). Fixed percentage increases, awarded randomly, tend to produce a distribution which is log-normal rather than normal: the bigger the base, the bigger the absolute effect of a percentage increase. For an intuitive explanation, see R. Marris, 'Towards a Reform of the Big Firm', *New Society*, Sept. 1969. For a more rigorous treatment, see *The Corporate Economy*, pp. 399–407.

An older attempt at a non-economic explanation of the growth of firms was Marshall's analogy with the trees of the forest (*Principles*, bk ɪᴠ, p. 263).

17. P. Sargent Florence, *Ownership, Control and Success of Large Companies* (London: Sweet & Maxwell 1971). Radice classified companies in which there was a definable interest group holding more than 15 per cent of the voting shares as owner-controlled, and those where the proportion was less than 5 per cent as management-controlled.

18. G. Whittington, 'The Profitability of Retained Earnings', *Review of Economics and Statistics* (May 1972). See also, on the subject of stock-market control, W. J. Baumol, *The Stock Market and Economic Efficiency* (New York: Fordham Univ. Press, 1965); and W. J. Baumol, P. Heim, B. G. Malkiel and R. E. Quandt, 'Earnings Retention, New Capital and the Growth of the Firm', *Review of Economics and Statistics* (Nov. 1970).

19. The logic of Whittington's argument is not too clear. It assumes diminishing marginal profitability of investment opportunities *over time* − so that, in a given, arbitrarily chosen time period, a firm is either setting off on a new burst of investments with a high rate of return, or is finishing off a series, begun in a previous period, by scraping the bottom of the opportunity barrel (or, alternatively, is somewhere in between). In that case, to select firms in either group will give a distorted picture of the effect of external financing on profitability in the next period. In any case the neoclassical assumption would be that during a given period of time the firm will be undertaking a gamut of projects ranging from those with a high rate of return to those (marginal ones) with a rate equal to the cost of capital. The average rate of return is naturally higher in those firms with higher rates on intra-marginal projects.

20. A. Singh, *Take-overs*, (Cambridge Univ. Press 1971) p. 11.

21. Ibid., p. 81.

22. D. A. Kuehn, 'Stock Market Valuation and Acquisitions: An Empirical Test of One Component of Managerial Utility', *Journal of Industrial Economics* (Apr. 1969).

8

SUMMARY AND CONCLUSIONS

THE models reviewed here are differentiated from each other chiefly by the character and complexity of the managerial utility function which is to be maximised. In the classical model the simplest assumption is made – that managers and owners have a joint utility function in which profit is the single argument. The models, except the classical model, are nevertheless homogeneous in that they all presuppose the exercise of managerial discretion in oligopolistic markets where inter-firm conflict is ignored as a significant factor in decision-making. It could therefore be claimed that they are relevant to a wide area of industrial activity.

Because the models make different behavioural assumptions they offer different behavioural predictions. None of the models should be termed general if this implies that it is useful for all occasions: a model which is useful for one purpose should be expected to be useless for another, and models for which general validity is claimed will run the risk of tolerating too high a level of abstraction. The managerial models are nevertheless more general than the profit-maximising model in the sense that they can be shown to include it as a special case while offering more fruitful approaches which it would ignore.

Managerial theories are thus more realistic in their assumptions and as a consequence they predict responses which in most cases are different from those of profit maximisers and closer to those found in reality. However, the managerial models are no more operational than entrepreneurial models: they are analytic rather than descriptive or prescriptive.

In particular, there are few concrete conclusions to be drawn on the pricing policies implied in the models. In the dynamic models pricing is very much in the background, although Marris has shown in chap. 4 of *Managerial Capitalism* how, depending on the type of diversification involved, pricing policies may diverge little from those required to maximise profits. Pricing problems are too difficult to solve with generality in a growth model: 'we are here forced to assume that the firm takes the best decisions in these respects of which it is capable'.[1] Superficially the Baumol static model implies full-cost pricing, particularly for the single-product case, but in fact the two approaches are by no means equivalent. In the case of the multi-product firm the relationship of sales maximising to full cost breaks down even more clearly: 'the equalities which follow from sales-maximisation are all marginal. They yield no simple pricing rule and certainly no average cost pricing rule.'[2] In both the Baumol and the O. E. Williamson static models price is assumed to be a decreasing function of output and an increasing function of administrative and selling expenses. A downward shift in demand reduces both output and selling expenses, and the effect on price is qualitatively uncertain. An increase in fixed cost might cause a price increase, but not necessarily. And in any case we are asked to suppose that the firm changes output in the first instance, with price varying contingently.

Managerial behaviour has welfare implications, particularly in relation to pricing and output policies, but generalisations cannot be made. It is possible that the hypothetically greater outputs and lower prices of managerial firms place us closer to an ideal use of resources, but this conclusion is extremely tentative. On balance the O. E. Williamson manager is likely to be less desirable than the Baumol manager since there is a greater likelihood of increases in prices as opposed to increases in output. This is because in the former case expansion of output is a derived response to the positive preference for an expansion of staff. If increasing staff tends to make the demand curve more inelastic, higher prices may result.[3]

Given certain simplifying assumptions, the growth rate will be unaffected by decisions about the relative amounts of finance which should be raised by new issues. Growth objectives can be pursued by means of retained earnings at the expense of dividends, but increased retentions have the dangerous effect of lowering the market valuation of the firm and increasing the danger of take-over. Whether the active variable is the dividend (as Lintner suggests) or the retention ratio, or the growth rate (as in Marris), the conclusion is that an optimal retention ratio is chosen so as to maximise safe growth. This ratio corresponds to Linter's target ratio (see above, p. 13), which may be a long-run equilibrium ratio towards which the firm moves but which it seldom achieves because in any one year only a partial adjustment in the direction of the target is attempted.

In a growth context the maximisation of profit becomes maximisation of the market valuation of the titles to ownership of the firm. In other words the market will judge whether growth through retentions or higher current income through dividends will increase shareholders' welfare more, and the effect of these judgements is seen in the valuation ratio. Maximising owners' welfare is by definition[4] then equivalent to maximising the valuation ratio, and it can be concluded that policies which are geared to maximising the welfare of managers will not achieve both objectives.

Macroeconomic implications of managerial theories are, like welfare implications, in principle manifold but in practice difficult to identify with precision. The famous tendency of sales maximisers to pass on lump-sum and profit taxes to consumers has fiscal and monetary consequences. But the most important potential influence is probably the effect that growth-oriented large firms could have on the rate of growth of the economy and therefore on the long-term welfare of society as a whole. Choice of a retention ratio which yields greater corporate savings than shareholders would voluntarily have made available may cause a long-run increase in the national propensity to save. Thus whereas in normal macroeconomic analysis equilibrium is achieved through some reconciliation of the propensities of savers and of investors, in a managerial system the investment decisions and saving decisions are to some extent in the same hands. Then the rate of macroeconomic growth could be affected by the growth policies of managers. In a recent article,[5] Marris has worked out a model which integrates his theory of the growth of firms with a neo-Keynesian macro-model. The result is that, among other things, as expected the more managerial the behaviour of firms, the higher the equilibrium macroeconomic growth rate.

On the evidence, few decisively measurable changes have taken place in the economic system as a result of a managerial revolution. Certainly its impact has been less apparent than that of either the industrial or the technological revolution. It would be more appropriate to call the occurrence an evolution rather than a revolution, but it is not a rate of change which is at issue, rather the extent and nature of change. It is clear that in those parts of the economic system organised into large corporations we no longer have, nor could have, traditional owner–managers, and that other forms of control have emerged. It is not established, though, that power over resources is precisely located with a definable managerial class, separated from the property-owning class; nor, consequently, can it be established beyond reasonable argument what goals managerial decision-makers have. Possibly this is purely a problem of definition and measurement: that is, an econometric problem. Some informed guesses have been discussed in the foregoing pages and most of them are fruitful in potential solutions. Yet there is still clearly tremendous scope for investigation into the goals and policies of both large and medium-sized firms.

Another possibility is that a counter-revolutionary drive by the combined forces of property and state is confronting the Berlian managers and undermining their attempt to set up a kind of uncontrolled trust for the administration of productive assets. The optimist of the Meade Lib-Lab variety would hope that such a combination could ensure democratic control of, as well as efficient use of, our resources. The pessimist might consider a more drastic solution unavoidable.

NOTES AND REFERENCES

1. R. L. Marris *The Economic Theory of 'Managerial' Capitalism*, p. 229.
2. Baumol, *Business Behavior, Value and Growth*, p. 66.
3. O. E. Williamson, *The Economics of Discretionary Behavior*, p. 169.
4. This assumes that a shareholder's utility function includes only the financial aspects of his shareholdings and does not embrace any interest in the non-financial implications of company policy.
5. R. L. Marris, 'Why Economics Needs a Theory of the Firm', *Economic Journal* (Mar. 1972).

BIBLIOGRAPHY

A. A. ALCHIAN, The Basis of Some Recent Advances in the Theory of Management of the Firm', *Journal of Industrial Economics* (Nov. 1965).

G. C. ALLEN, *Economic Fact and Fantasy* (Institute of Economic Affairs Occasional Paper No. 14 1969).

R. G. D. ALLEN, *Mathematical Analysis for Economists* (London: Macmillan, 1938).

P. W. S. ANDREWS, *Manufacturing Business* (London: Macmillan, 1949).

G. C. ARCHIBALD, 'The Comparative Statics of Monopolistic Competition', in G. C. Archibald (ed.), *The Theory of the Firm* (Harmondsworth: Penguin Books, 1971).

A. G. ARMSTRONG and A. SILBERSTON, 'Size of Plant, Size of Enterprise and Concentration in British Manufacturing Industry 1935–58', *Journal of the Royal Statistical Society*, vol. CXXVIII, pt 3 (1965).

W. L. BALDWIN, 'The Motives of Managers, Environmental Restraints, and the Theory of Managerial Enterprise', *Quarterly Journal of Economics* (May 1964).

W. J. BAUMOL, *Business Behavior, Value and Growth* (New York: Macmillan, 1959).

—— 'On the Theory of Expansion of the Firm', *American Economic Review* (Dec. 1962).

—— *The Stock Market and Economic Efficiency* (New York: Fordham Univ. Press, 1965).

—— P. HEIM, B. G. MALKIEL and R. E. QUANDT, 'Earnings Retention, New Capital and the Growth of the Firm', *Review of Economics and Statistics* (Nov. 1970).

—— and M. STEWART, 'On the Behavioral Theory of the Firm', in R. L. Marris and A. J. B. Woods (eds.), *The Corporate Economy* (London: Macmillan, 1971).

C. S. BEED, 'The Separation of Ownership from Control', *Journal of Economic Studies*, vol. I, no. 2 (1966).

A. A. BERLE and G. C. MEANS, *The Modern Corporation and Private Property* (New York: Harcourt, Brace & World, 1932; rev. ed., 1967).

E. H. CHAMBERLIN, *The Theory of Monopolistic Competition* (Oxford Univ. Press, 1933).

G. P. E. CLARKSON (ed.), *Managerial Economics* (Harmondsworth: Penguin Books, 1968).

C. A. R. CROSLAND, *The Future of Socialism*, rev. ed. (London: Cape, 1964).

—— 'The Private and Public Corporation in Great Britain', in E. S. Mason (ed.), *The Corporation in Modern Society* (Cambridge, Mass.: Harvard Univ. Press, 1959).

R. M. CYERT and K. D. GEORGE, 'Competition, Growth and Efficiency', *Economic Journal* (Mar. 1969).

—— and J. G. MARCH, *A Behavioral Theory of the Firm* (Englewood Cliffs, N.J.: Prentice-Hall, 1963).

R. DORFMAN, 'An Economic Interpretation of Optimal Control Theory', *American Economic Review* (Dec. 1969).

P. SARGANT FLORENCE, *Ownership, Control and Success of Large Companies* (London: Sweet & Maxwell, 1961).

M. FRIEDMAN, *Essays in Positive Economics* (Univ. of Chicago Press, 1953).

J. K. GALBRAITH, *The New Industrial State* (London: Hamish Hamilton, 1967).

K. D. GEORGE, *Industrial Organisation* (London: Allen & Unwin, 1972).

M. GORDON, *The Investment, Financing and Valuation of the Corporation* (Homewood, Ill.: Irwin, 1962).

H. G. GRABOWSKI and D. C. MUELLER, 'Managerial and Stockholder Welfare Models of Firm Expenditure', *Review of Economics and Statistics* (Feb. 1972).

M. HALL, 'Sales Revenue Maximisation: An Empirical Examination', *Journal of Industrial Economics* (Apr. 1967); 'Reply', ibid. (Nov. 1968).

P. E. HART, 'The Size and Growth of Firms', *Economica* (Feb. 1962).

R. HAVEMAN and G. DEBARTOLO, 'The Revenue Maximising Oligopoly Model: A Comment', *American Economic Review* (Dec. 1968); 'Reply', ibid. (June 1970).

C. J. HAWKINS, 'On the Sales Revenue Maximisation Hypothesis, *Journal of Industrial Economics* (Apr. 1970).

—— 'The Revenue Maximisation Oligopoly Model: Comment', *American Economic Review* (June 1970).

G. M. HEAL and A. SILBERSTON, 'Alternative Managerial Objectives: An Explanatory Note', *Oxford Economic Papers* (July 1972).

J. M. HENDERSON and R. E. QUANDT, *Microeconomic Theory* (New York: McGraw-Hill, 1958).

J. R. HICKS, *Value and Capital*, 2nd ed. (Oxford Univ. Press, 1946).

—— *Capital and Growth* (Oxford Univ. Press, 1965).

I. HOROWITZ, *Decision Making and the Theory of the Firm* (New York: Holt, Rinehart & Winston, 1970).

M. Z. KAFOGLIS and R. C. BUSHNELL, 'The Revenue Maximisation Oligopoly Model: Comment', *American Economic Review* (June 1970).

C. KAYSEN, 'The Social Significance of the Modern Corporation', *American Economic Asssociation Papers and Proceedings* (May 1957).

—— 'Another View of Corporate Capitalism', *Quarterly Journal of Economics* (Feb. 1965).

L. R. KLEIN *et al.*, 'Savings and Finances of the Upper Income Classes', *Bulletin of the Oxford Institute of Statistics* (Nov. 1956).

O. KNAUTH, *Managerial Enterprise: Its Growth and Methods of Operations* (New York: W. W. Norton, 1948).

D. A. KUEHN, 'Stock Market Valuation and Acquisitions: An Empirical Test of One Component of Managerial Utility, *Journal of Industrial Economics* (Apr. 1969).

H. W. KUHN and A. TUCKER, 'Nonlinear Programming' in J. Neyman (ed.), *Proceedings of the Second Berkeley Symposium on Mathematical Statistics and Probability* (Berkeley: Univ. of California Press, 1951).

R. J. LARNER, 'The Two Hundred Largest Non-Financial Corporations', *American Economic Review* (Sept. 1966).

R. H. LEFTWICH, *The Price System and Resource Allocation*, 4th ed. (New York: Holt, Rinehart & Winston, 1970).

H. LEIBENSTEIN, 'Allocative Efficiency versus X-Efficiency', *American Economic Review* (June 1966).

W. G. LEWELLEN, *The Ownership Income of Management* (New York: Columbia Univ. Press, 1971).

J. LINTNER, 'The Financing of Corporations', in E. S. Mason (ed.), *The Corporation in Modern Society* (Cambridge, Mass.: Harvard Univ. Press, 1959).

—— 'Distribution of Incomes of Corporations among Dividends, Retained Earnings and Taxes', *American Economic Association, Papers and Proceedings* (May 1956).

—— 'Optimum or Maximum Corporate Growth under Uncertainty' in R. L. Marris and A. J. B. Woods (eds.), *The Corporate Economy* (London: Macmillan, 1971).

R. G. LIPSEY and P. O. STEINER, *Economics* (New York: Harper & Row, 1966).

J. W. McGUIRE, J. S. Y. CHIU and A. O. ELBING, 'Executive Incomes, Sales and Profits', American Economic Review (Sept. 1962).

F. MACHLUP, 'Theories of the Firm', American Economic Review (Mar. 1967). Reprinted in D. Needham (ed.), Readings in the Economics of Industrial Organisation (New York: Holt, Rinehart & Winston, 1970).

J. G. MARCH and H. A. SIMON, Organisations (New York: Wiley, 1958).

R. L. MARRIS, The Economic Theory of 'Managerial' Capitalism (London: Macmillan, 1964).

—— 'Towards a Reform of the Big Firm', New Society, (Sept. 1969).

—— 'Why Economics Needs a Theory of the Firm', Economic Journal (Mar. 1972).

—— and A. J. B. WOOD (eds.), The Corporate Economy (London: Macmillan, 1971).

A. MARSHALL, Principles of Economics, 8th ed. (London: Macmillan, 1920).

E. S. MASON, 'The Apologetics of Managerialism', Journal of Business (Jan. 1958).

—— (ed.), The Corporation in Modern Society (Cambridge, Mass.: Harvard Univ. Press, 1959).

J. E. MEADE, 'Is "The New Industrial State" Inevitable?', Economic Journal (June 1968).

J. MEYER and E. KUH, The Investment Decision (Cambridge, Mass.: Harvard Univ. Press, 1957).

F. MODIGLIANI and M. MILLER, 'The Cost of Capital, Corporation Finance and the Theory of Investment', American Economic Review (June 1958).

T. H. NAYLOR and J. M. VERNON, Microeconomics and Decision Models of the Firm (New York: Harcourt, Brace & World, 1969).

D. NEEDHAM, Economic Analysis and Industrial Structure (New York: Holt, Rinehart & Winston, 1969).

—— (ed.), Readings in the Economics of Industrial Organisation (New York: Holt, Rinehart & Winston, 1970).

T. NICHOLS, Ownership, Control and Ideology (London: Allen & Unwin, 1969).

D. K. OSBORNE, 'On the Goals of the Firm', Quarterly Journal of Economics (Nov. 1964).

E. T. PENROSE, The Theory of the Growth of the Firm (Oxford: Blackwell, 1959).

M. H. PESTON, 'On the Sales Maximisation Hypothesis', Economica (May 1959).

A. PHILLIPS, 'An Attempt to Synthesise some Theories of the Firm', in A. Phillips and O. E. Williamson (eds.), Prices: Issues in Theory, Practice and Public Policy (Oxford Univ. Press, 1969).

H. K. RADICE, 'Control Type, Profitability and Growth in Large Firms: An Empirical Study', Economic Journal (Sept. 1971).

W. B. REDDAWAY, 'An Analysis of Take-overs', Lloyds Bank Review (Apr. 1972).

D. R. ROBERTS, Executive Compensation (Glencoe, Ill.: Free Press, 1959).

H. B. ROSE and G. D. NEWBOULD, 'The 1967 Take-over Boom', Moorgate and Wall Street (autumn 1967).

E. V. ROSTOW, 'To Whom is Corporate Management Responsible?', in E. S. Mason (ed.), The Corporation in Modern Society (Cambridge, Mass.: Harvard Univ. Press, 1959).

C. K. ROWLEY and M. A. CREW, 'Anti-Trust Policy: Economics versus Management Science', Moorgate and Wall Street (autumn 1970).

J. M. SAMUELS (ed.), Readings on Mergers and Take-overs (London: Paul Elek, 1972).

P. A. SAMUELSON, Foundations of Economic Analysis (Cambridge, Mass.: Harvard Univ. Press, 1948).

R. L. SANDMEYER, 'Baumol's Sales Maximisation Model', American Economic Review (Dec. 1964).

W. G. SHEPHERD, 'On Sales Maximising and Oligopoly Behaviour', Economica (Nov. 1962).

H. A. SIMON, 'Theories of Decision Making in Economics and the Behavioral Sciences, *American Economic Review* (June 1959).
—— 'New Developments in the Theory of the Firm', *American Economic Association, Papers and Proceedings* (May 1962).
A. SINGH, *Take-overs* (Cambridge Univ. Press, 1971).
—— and G. WHITTINGTON, *Growth, Profitability and Valuation* (Cambridge Univ. Press, 1968).
D. J. SMYTH, 'Sales Maximisation and Managerial Effort: Note', *American Economic Review* (Sept. 1969).
G. J. STIGLER, 'The Kinky Oligopoly Demand Curve and Rigid Prices', *Journal of Political Economy* (Oct. 1947).
D. VILLAREJO, 'Stock Ownership and the Control of Corporations', *New University Thought* (Chicago, 1961, 1962).
L. WAVERMAN, 'Sales Revenue Maximisation: A Note', *Journal of Industrial Economics* (Nov. 1968).
G. WHITTINGTON, 'The Profitability of Retained Earnings', *Review of Economics and Statistics* (May 1972).
P. J. WILES, *Price, Cost and Output* (Oxford Univ. Press, 1956).
J. H. WILLIAMSON, 'Profit, Growth and Sales Maximisation', *Economica* (Feb. 1966). Reprinted in G. C. Archibald (ed.), *The Theory of the Firm* (Harmondsworth: Penguin Books, 1971) and in D. Needham (ed.), *Readings in the Economics of Industrial Organisation* (New York: Holt, Rinehart & Winston, 1970).
O. E. WILLIAMSON, 'A Dynamic Stochastic Theory of Managerial Behavior', in A. Phillips and O. E. Williamson (eds.), *Prices: Issues in Theory, Practice and Public Policy* (Oxford Univ. Press, 1969).
—— *The Economics of Discretionary Behavior* (Chicago: Markham, 1967).
—— *Corporate Control and Business Behavior* (Englewood Cliffs, N.J.: Prentice-Hall, 1970).

GLOSSARY OF SYMBOLS

THE symbols listed are used as consistently as possible throughout in the sense given. Occasionally the connotation of a symbol changes slightly from model to model. Occasionally letters have been used for other purposes, for example in diagrams, but in such cases no ambiguity should arise. Consistency of notation has often made it necessary to abandon the notation used by the original authors.

a = constant marginal cost of growth
C = cost (usually production cost)
d = dividend
$D(g)$ = dividend function
E = condition of the environment
f = growth rate of equity
F = equity
g = growth rate
g_d = growth rate of dividend
G = costs of expansion or growth
i = rate of interest or discount rate
K = capital
M = market value of firm [or managerial emoluments in the Williamson model]
$\underline{p}$ = rate of return or rate of profit (reported profit) = π/K
$\bar{p}$ = operating profit rate
π = total profit
π_0 = minimum acceptable profit
P = price of product
r = retention ratio
R = total revenue or sales
S = expenditure on staff or sales promotion
t = profit-tax rate
$\bar{T}$ = lump-sum tax
T = tax − either profit tax or lump-sum tax
U = utility
v = valuation ratio = M/K
v_{im} = market valuation ratio of ith firm
v_{ij} = raider j's valuation ratio for ith firm
$\bar{v}$ = constrained minimum value of v
w = proportion of its potential maximum value below which the management feels it could not safely allow the market value to fall
X = output
y_1, y_2 = coefficients in Marris linear model
$Y(g)$ = present value function = $1/(i − g)$

INDEX

advertising
  in Baumol model   44, 46, 48, 57, 61
  demand growth and   108
  effectiveness of   47, 90
  marginal revenue of   46–48, 57
  and price decisions   48–52
  tax   17
  wastefulness of   17
Alchian A. A.   61, 67
allocative efficiency   27, 34
Andrews P. W. S.   53, 67
annual meeting   7, 8, 20
anti-monopoly action, need for   83
Armstrong A. G.   3, 20
aspiration level   25, 26
asset growth   5, 12, 61, 90
  balanced   86, 100
asset maximisation   61

bandwaggoning   112
Baumol W. J.   1, 21, 26, 29, 126, 128
  on financial policy   14, 15, 124
  on growth   101
  model   42–67
    and traditional model   30–41
    and O. E. Williamson model   70–81
Beed C. S.   7, 8, 21
behavioural theory   26, 27
Berle A. A.   2, 6, 7, 12–15, 18–22, 68, 128
bonds   12, 93
bonus schemes   115
book value   87, 96, 117

calculus of variations   86
capital
  cost of   12, 87, 88, 98, 124
  equipment   33, 88
  as a factor of production   15, 16, 21, 22
  gain   9, 14, 93, 97, 100, 105
  market
    control by   6–12
    and financial policy   12–15, 92
    and growth policy   100–105, 117
    and minimum profit level   43
    and take-over   106
  stock   87, 91, 101, 102
capital-output ratio   90, 102, 107, 113
capitalism   1, 2, 33
  corporate   32, 82, 84, 106

chain reaction   108–112
Chamberlin E. H.   38, 41
class   2, 5, 20, 109, 110, 128
classical model   33–37, 125
  of demand   107
  and growth model   84, 85
  and managerial models   80, 82
  of market valuation   114
  and organisation theory   23
classical growth rate   119
coalition   23–26
comparative statics
  competitive model   34
  discretion model   74–80
  monopoly   35
  sales maximising model   56
competition
  in capital market   6, 43, 117
  perfect   33–35, 38–40, 81
  in product market   17, 28, 43, 117
competitive pressure   88, 102
concentration   2, 3
conjectural variation   36, 37, 42
consumer
  behaviour   17, 107–112
  preference   16, 107
convergence   94, 95, 103
control   6
  separation of ownership and   1–20, 128
  loss   82
  theory   22
corporate conscience   2, 15–20, 68, 106
cost
  expansion   32, 88–92, 97, 98
  fixed, increase in   35, 36, 43, 56, 58, 80, 126
  marginal
    and marginal revenue   40, 44, 46, 49, 63, 73, 78, 79
    and price   34, 37, 40, 58
  operating   62, 88–90, 98
  reduction   17, 27, 81
  as side payment   23
  social   16
  variable   52–58
costing margin   53, 54
Cournot A.   37
criticality   109, 110
Crosland C. A. R.   16, 19, 22

cross section analysis 81, 102
Cyert R. M. 1, 20–29, 62

De Bartolo G. 50, 56, 66, 67
debt 14, 92, 93, 102
demand
  decrease in 81, 126
  elasticity
    and demand shift 81, 126
    and full cost 54, 55
    in monopoly 35
    perfect 89
    and sales maximising 45, 64, 65
    of saturated product
  growth 91, 92, 107, 113, 117, 118
    function 112, 119
  increase in 34, 35, 53, 56
  long run 61
  theory 32, 107
demand curve 33, 54, 56, 81
  kinked 63, 64
  Marshallian 107, 123
  and welfare 58
determinism 17, 42
development cost 88, 96, 110, 117 f
directors 3–8, 11, 13, 20, 105
discount rate 9, 87, 95, 105, 106, 118, 123
discounting 32, 102, 103
discretion model 68
diversification 32 f, 89–92
  and growth 107–112
dividend 8, 9, 126, 127
  discriminatory taxes on 17, 97, 104
  function 113, 117, 118
  growth 87, 93–99, 103
  and minimum profit level 43
  policy 12–15, 92–101, 105
  and share price 85
Dorfman R. 22
dynamic constraints 90 f, 118
dynamics 1, 30–32, 84, 107

earnings
  corporate, as influence on dividend
    policy 13–15
  to shareholders 43
economic
  man 1, 24
  power 2, 16
  system 31, 84, 127
  theory 22, 24
economies of scale 33, 34
economists 1, 33, 68, 81

effort-aversion 64, 65
emoluments 69, 70, 78–81
empirical evidence
  for managerial discretion 68, 81
  for Marris model 119–123
  for sales maximising 64
employees 16–19, 23, 28, 70
entrepreneur 2, 16, 23, 38, 69, 71
entrepreneurial supply price 70
environment 14, 16, 25, 26, 86, 88, 92
  in Williamson model 70–83
equilibrium conditions 30, 31
  in competitive model 34, 39
  in Marris model 116
  in monopolistic competition 37
  in monopoly 35, 40
  in sales maximising model 44, 45, 50, 64
  in Williamson model 68, 71–74, 78, 80
excess capacity 34
executives 5, 13, 42, 65
expense preference 69, 78
explosion 110, 111
external finance 12, 91, 93, 120, 121, 124

finance supply curve 106
financial policy 2, 7, 12–15, 92,–101, 105
  optimal 92, 93, 97, 101
fiscal policy 60
Florence P. S. 3, 5, 21, 120, 124
full cost 52–56, 126

Galbraith J. K. 15–22, 85, 101
game theory 37, 42, 112
gearing 10, 92, 93, 102
geometric progression 94
George K. D. 20, 29, 102
gestation 110, 111
giant firms 22, 107, 123
Gibrat's Law 123
Gordon M. 119, 123
growth 84 f
  autonomous 89
  balanced 100, 107
  classical 119
  differentiated 107–112
  and discount rate 95
  diseconomies of 33, 118
  economies of 102
  goal 85, 120
  imitative 107, 111–112
  immanent 118, 119
  industry 117
  managerial 119, 123

growth—(*contd.*)
  marginal cost of   99, 118, 119
  marginal utility of   116, 117
  Marris model of   104–124
  maximising   85, 98–101, 114, 119, 126
  maximum safe   104, 114, 126
  minimum safe   114
  and profitability   84–88, 111–113, 119, 120
  rate of
    and take-over   105–107
    and valuation   113–119
    steady state   31, 86–89, 93, 100 f, 112
      optimum   97
    sustainable   93, 107
growth-profitability function   112, 113, 117
growth-stock paradox   95
growth-valuation function   113, 118

Hall, M.   62, 67
Haveman R.   50, 56, 66, 67
Hessian   39
Hicks J. R.   31, 40, 77

imperfect markets   6, 43, 93, 97
income effect   77, 78, 81
industrial revolution   127
independent preferences   108
inferior good   52, 77, 78
initial output   92, 102
initial size   102
innovation   112
input prices   27, 31, 39, 89
institutional investors   6
interest rate   93–101
integral   103
internal finance   12, 88–93, 96–101, 121
intrinsic utility   111
inventory goal   24
investment
  criteria   82
  policy   42, 43, 87
  project   87, 88, 93, 97, 124
  trust   6
iso-cost   51
iso-revenue   51
iso-valuation   99, 100

joint stock company   33, 86

Kahn formula   103
Kaysen C.   18, 22
Knauth O.   7, 21
Kuehn D. A.   122, 124

Kuh E.   119, 123
Kuhn–Tucker conditions   44, 72

labour   16, 28
labour force – see employees
Lagrangean   39, 44
land   15
latent need   108, 111
least cost behaviour   69, 82
Leibenstein H.   29, 34
leisure   16, 28, 65
Lewellen W. G.   5, 6, 21
Lib-Lab   128
linear homogeneity   41, 89
  model   118, 119, 123
  suburb   109
Lintner J.   12, 14, 20, 21, 26
liquidity   10
lump sum tax
  on competitive firm   35
  on monopolist   36
  on sales maximiser   44, 56, 57, 60, 127
  on utility maximiser   72, 74, 76, 78, 80
macroeconomics   27, 84, 127
Malthus T.   15
management control   6, 7, 120, 121, 124
managerial
  behaviour   2, 68, 98, 104, 126
  discretion   1, 6, 11, 32–35, 37, 88, 121, 125
    model   68–83
  diseconomies   33, 118
  efficiency   11, 105, 106, 113
  effort   64, 65
  goals   1, 15–22, 32, 37, 68, 69, 127
    evidence on   61–65, 81 f, 119 f
  income   4, 62, 65
  indifference curve   71, 77, 78, 83, 116
  insecurity   100, 101
  mobility   116
  ownership   3, 5, 116
  power   65, 68, 69, 115, 116
  revolution   15, 16, 127
  team   87–90, 100, 111, 116
  utility   20, 31, 64, 70, 82, 104, 115–117, 125
March J. G.   1, 23–29, 62
marginal cost – see cost
marginal revenue
  discontinuity in   63, 64
  equal to marginal cost   39, 49, 64, 73, 78, 79
  less than marginal cost   46

marginalism 53, 59, 60
market
    forces 11, 17–19
    population 109, 110
    price 34, 35
    shares goal 24
    value of firm 5, 10–15, 32, 86–88, 94–98,
        113–115
        maximisation of 85, 119, 127
        maximum 100, 114, 117
        minimum safe 100, 104, 106, 114, 122
marketing 31, 59, 108
    outlay 88 f, 117, 126
mark-up 30, 54, 58
Marris R. L. 1, 37, 38, 89, 93, 125–128
    on dynamics 32
    on managerial ownership 5
    model 104–124
Marshall A. 34, 41, 123, 124
Marxist argument 22
McGuire J. W. 62, 67
Meade J. E. 17, 22, 85, 102, 128
Means G. C. 2, 20–22
merger 11, 33
Meyer J. 119, 123
Miller M. 97, 103
minimum profit level – see profit constraint
minority control 6
microeconomics 33, 60, 84
M-firm 82
Modigliani F. 97, 103
monopolistic competition 37, 38
monopolistic market 6, 43, 82
monopoly 35–37, 40, 59, 70, 113
    output 45, 58
multiproduct firm 89, 126

needs 108
neo-classical behaviour 30, 57, 82, 120
neo-classical theory 27, 30–41, 117, 119,
    124
Newbould G. D. 11, 20, 21
non-pecuniary goals 69

oligopolistic behaviour 42, 43, 63
oligopoly 27, 36, 52, 60–63, 81, 89, 125
    interdependence in 37, 42, 63
opportunity cost 9, 23, 34, 43, 88, 95, 98
optimisation 30, 53–55, 65
organisation
    goal 23, 24
    man 24
    theory 1, 23–29, 68

Osborne D. K. 66
output
    fixer 52
    goal 28
    growth 16, 86–92, 100, 102, 107
    with kinked demand 63
    welfare 58, 59
output-oriented firm 62
overheads 52
owner control 120, 121, 124
owner-managers 128
owners 3–8, 18, 23, 43, 82, 117
ownership 1–8, 105
Oxford Institute of Statistics 5, 21

Pareto V. 58, 60
payout 13, 97, 105
    ratio 14, 93, 100
Penrose E. T. 85, 102
Penrose effect 90, 91, 99, 102, 113, 118
perpetual bond 95
perfect competition 33–35, 40, 41, 81
perquisites 31, 69, 70
Peston M. H. 61, 62, 67
pioneers 108–110
planning 17, 18
policy commitment 23, 24
Pontryagin L. S. 22
Prais S. J. 3
present value 85, 94, 99, 102
    function 95, 113, 117, 118
prestige 43, 65, 68, 69, 115, 116
price
    competition 64
    demand as a function of 36, 44, 72, 107,
        126
    equal to marginal cost 34, 40, 58
    fixer 52
    greater than marginal cost 37
    increase after tax 35–38, 56–58
    with kinked demand 63, 64
    mechanism 17, 18
    taker 33, 40
pricing policy 24, 42, 48–58, 81, 110, 125
primary group 109, 110
problemistic search 25
product differentiation 18, 38, 81, 89, 107
production
    function 27, 38, 41, 89
    goal 24
productivity 102, 120
profit
    abnormal 28, 35, 37, 43

profit —*(contd.)*
  average 111
  constraint
    Baumol 42–66
    Williamson 70–72, 78, 79
  current 85, 87, 100, 101
  discretionary 70–72, 80, 83
  function 56, 57, 63, 71, 77, 78
  goal 24, 28, 68, 82, 84
  and growth 84–91
  margin 46, 52–55
  marginal utility of 83
  maximum 43, 53, 60, 82, 87, 99, 111
  normal 35, 53
  operating 88, 89, 118, 119
  rate 96 f
  reported 70, 79, 86–88, 96, 98, 118 f
  steady growth of 112
  tax
    on sales-maximiser 43, 57
    on traditional firm 35, 36
    on utility maximiser 71–80, 127
  undistributed 85
profit maximising 33–40
  advertising level 47, 48, 52
  and growth 84–88, 98 f
  growth rate 99, 100
  long run 61, 62
  and managerial utility 116, 117
  output 39, 46, 52, 54, 58, 60, 62
  price 34, 36, 111, 126
  retentions 99, 100
profitability
  and growth 112
  marginal 121, 124
professional etiquette 42
professional excellence 68, 69
property 2–5, 128
proxy machinery 7–9, 13
  variable 31, 116

quadratic forms 39
quality 102, 123
quoted companies 10, 104

Radice 120, 123, 124
raider 9, 105
  most dangerous 106
rate of return 9, 96 f, 123, 124
  average 104, 124
  and growth rate 119
  marginal 88, 104
  and retentions 120

rate of return—*(contd.)*
  and take-over 11, 105–107
  and valuation 114–121
rate of technical substitution 39
reinvestment 14, 43
rent 6, 34, 70, 79
rentier 3
representative firm 34, 102
research 17, 32, 91, 117
retention ratio 10, 14, 98
  and growth rate 119
  and rate of return 120
  and valuation 114–118
retentions 12–15, 92, 98 f, 126, 127
return discrepancy ratio 103
revenue – see sales
Ricardo D. 15
risk 93
risk-aversion 118
Roberts D. R. 62, 67, 123
Rose H. B. 11, 20, 21
Rostow E. V. 6, 8, 9, 21
rule-of-thumb 27, 42, 52–55, 60

safety condition 106
salary 5, 23, 43, 68–70, 115, 116
sales
  constrained 45, 46, 47
  current 61, 85, 100, 101
  function 49, 56, 62–64
  goal 24, 43, 120
  growth 84, 89–92, 101, 112
  maximum 45, 60, 63
  preferred to profit 61, 62
  tax 35, 36, 38, 57
sales maximising
  advertising level 47–52, 56, 60
  equilibrium 45, 46, 48–51
  model 42–65
  output 45, 46, 49, 50, 51, 54, 56–60
  price 48–50
  profit 46, 49
Samuelson P. A. 30–32, 40
Sandmeyer R. L. 48–50, 66
satisfying 26, 30
saturation 110–112
savings 3, 12, 127
scale 33, 35, 62
  diseconomies of 33
  economies of 33, 34
  and growth 86 f
  optimum 34, 37, 90
  and take-over 10, 106

secondary group 110
security 42 f, 68 f, 91, 106, 115 f, 122
security constraint 114
shadow price 60
shares 3–5
  issues of 12–15, 85, 92–98, 102, 126
  number of 96
  price of 14, 20, 85, 91, 97, 105
  selling of 8, 105
shareholder 4–15, 18–20, 23, 85, 94, 127
  committee 8
  new 97
  orientation of management 20, 100, 106
  preferences 14, 21, 43, 88, 105, 128
  welfare 14, 15, 84, 97, 114, 117, 127
sheep 108
Shepherd W. G. 63, 64, 67
side payments 23, 24
Silberston A. 3, 20, 102
Singh A. 9, 11, 21, 120—123
size distribution 106, 120, 123
Smyth D. J. 64, 67
social
  barrier 110
  benefit 34
  class 109
  service 15 f, 68
socio-economic contact 109
Solow R. M. 101–103
staff 31, 44, 62, 126
  marginal revenue product of 73, 76
  marginal utility of 75, 78
  model 69–83
state 18, 20, 83, 128
static
  constraints 90
  equilibrium 102
  market 111, 112
statics 1, 30–33, 84
status 31, 65–69
stock
  exchange 10
  market 5, 6, 88, 92, 113–116, 119
  option 5, 115, 116
  voting 6–9
stockholder suit 8
stratification 110
substitution effect 77, 78, 80

supply, elasticity of 106, 116
survival 69, 82

take-over 8–12, 104–107, 117, 122, 126
take-over code 9
target ratio 13, 14, 21, 126, 127
technical progress 62
technocracy 18
technological revolution 16, 127
technostructure 15–17, 84
trade union 23
transaction costs 97, 98, 104
transformation curve 115
trees of the forest 124

U-firm 82
uncertainty 11, 15, 25, 82 f, 93 f, 100, 118
unprofitable outlets 62
utility function
  managerial 20, 32, 64, 125
  Marris 115–117
  Williamson 70, 72, 77, 82, 83

valuation
  curve 113–117
  formula 97, 103, 105
  ratio 86, 87, 96, 98, 123, 127
    and managerial utility 114–117
    and take-over 10, 105–107, 122
value judgement 2, 16
vicarious experience 108
Villarejo D. 3, 21
volume maximising 110

wages 16, 23
want creation 108
wants 108, 123
wealth 2, 3, 5, 7, 61
welfare 16, 60
welfare implications 35, 58, 59, 81, 126, 127
Whittington G. 120–124
Williamson J. H. 32, 41, 93, 97, 100, 101
Williamson O. E. 1, 7, 9, 11, 31, 62, 126
  model 68–83
  on organisation theory 26–30
Wood A. J. B. 27, 32, 102
work ethic 65

X-efficiency 27, 28, 34, 119